CHECKED AND BALANCED

▲

To Roger

with best wishes from
his warrior friend and to
say "congratulations for 10
years" for Fox News —

Jauce
10/30/06

CHECKED AND BALANCED

*How Ticket-Splitters Are Shaping
the New Balance of Power
in American Politics*

V. Lance Tarrance, Jr., and Walter De Vries
with Donna L. Mosher

WILLIAM B. EERDMANS PUBLISHING COMPANY
GRAND RAPIDS, MICHIGAN / CAMBRIDGE, U.K.

© 1998 Wm. B. Eerdmans Publishing Co.
255 Jefferson Ave. S.E., Grand Rapids, Michigan 49503 /
P.O. Box 163, Cambridge CB3 9PU U.K.

Printed in the United States of America

03 02 01 00 99 98   7 6 5 4 3 2 1

Library of Congress Cataloging-in-Publication Data

Tarrance, V. Lance.
Checked and balanced: how ticket-splitters are shaping
the new balance of power in American politics /
V. Lance Tarrance and Walter De Vries with Donna Mosher.
p.   cm.
Includes index.
ISBN 0-8028-4593-2 (paper: alk. paper)
1. Party affiliation — United States. 2. Voting — United States.
3. Presidents — United States — Election — 1996.
4. United States. Congress — Elections, 1996.
I. De Vries, Walter. II. Mosher, Donna L. III. Title.
JK2271.T37 1998

324.973′0929 — dc21   98-27422
                                                    CIP

To our fathers,
V. Lance Tarrance, Sr. and Martin De Vries,
both in the ninth decades of their lives,
who have witnessed the enormous political
and governmental changes
of the twentieth century

Contents

Foreword

Of all the interviews quoted in this book, the one that cut deepest into my consciousness was that of the Michigan woman who said she thought the system of government ordained by the Founders "was set up to balance power. . . . One party control is almost anti-American."

That comment goes to the heart of this book, and it is a heavy blow to those of us who have argued for years that party responsibility is necessary for strong government performance and for accountability to voters.

A full generation ago, a critical mass of American voters came to believe that straight-ticket voting, the prevailing pattern in our previous national history, was foolish, self-limiting, "almost anti-American."

The first people to document this phenomenon were V. Lance Tarrance, Jr., and Walter De Vries in their 1972 book, *The Ticket-Splitter*. In this volume, a quarter-century later, they describe how ticket-splitting has evolved into government-splitting and how the new pattern of power sharing has forced both Republicans and Democrats into what they call "competitive cooperation."

It is a bold analysis. They are even bolder in predicting that public support for this new pattern of politics is so strong that it is likely to become the prevailing pattern in this new era of American history. But given the prescience of their earlier volume, their view is not one to be dismissed.

The evidence begins with the well-documented persistence of the ticket-splitting pattern they described in their first book. (Here and elsewhere, the term refers to people who voted for a president of one party and a member of the House from another party.) The authors' pre-election survey in 1996 and the Gallup post-election poll indicate about one-fifth of the electorate were ticket-splitters. That number has been holding steady for a generation. But more than three times as many told the Roper Center pollsters in 1996 that they "typically" shun straight-ticket voting. That 70 percent of those polled make that claim is probably best understood as a measure of the social stigma that now attaches to that "old-fashioned" way of voting.

With Republicans and Democrats now essentially tied in their core support, the ticket-splitters are clearly numerous enough to swing the balance of power in national elections.

Are they seeking divided government? De Vries and Tarrance offer an equivocal answer to that question — which is the critical second step of their argument.

As they explain in Chapter 2, the post-election Gallup survey found only 2 out of 100 voters who said they had split their tickets deliberately for the purpose of balancing their vote and creating divided government. That is a very small fraction on which to rest a large theory about a new era of politics and government. But, as they point out, there are forces in the environment that suggest that this way of thinking is far more pervasive than the 2 percent figure would suggest — and is likely to increase.

One is the increase in the percentage of Americans who say they prefer divided government. Between 1992 and 1997, one pair of surveys they cite suggests, the public preference shifted from four-to-three in favor of one-party government to a similar ratio preferring split control.

Second is the increasing familiarity — and presumably comfort — Americans have with the fact of divided government. In the fifty-six years from 1893 to 1949, we had forty-six years of one-party government in Washington. Of the fifty years since, only twenty have seen a single party simultaneously in control of the White House, the Senate, and the House. In the same fifty years, the number of states with divided government has increased from eighteen to thirty-one. If trends this strong are not reflective of a change in public preference, then the voters are cursed with a half-century of perversely bad luck.

The final step of the Tarrance–De Vries argument, begun in Chapter 1 and extended to its logical conclusion in Chapter 6, is that divided government works well and reflects a new popular understanding of the Founders' design.

As the authors point out, the view of a previous generation of political scientists was that the political parties emerged in America to provide the necessary bridges across the division of powers created by the Constitution. The dominant academic voices said that only when there was a clear designation of one party with responsibility for both the legislative and executive branches was there the impetus for cooperation that could generate significant governmental action. Otherwise, they said, the checks and balances of the Constitution would naturally produce policy gridlock.

That view was natural enough for scholars who had seen Franklin Roosevelt and a series of Democratic Congresses combine to produce a wealth of New Deal economic and social legislation. The same pairing cooperated in the decisions that prepared America for World War II and mobilized the nation for victory. Cheering activist government, as did most Americans at the time, these scholars understandably saw strong and clear party responsibility as the precondition for its success.

It was David Mayhew of Yale who first challenged that orthodoxy in his 1991 book, *Divided We Govern*. He examined the legislative output of Congresses in periods of divided government and argued that they were at least as productive as those in unified government — and in some instances, more so.

When I encountered Professor Mayhew at a political science convention shortly after his book was published, I confessed that I was suffering acute mental pain because of his powerful challenge to the doctrine of responsible party government I had absorbed years before at the University of Chicago and had regurgitated in a book of my own, *The Party's Over*.

Grasping for straws, I asked Mayhew how he explained the meager output we were seeing from the current government, with Republican George Bush in the White House and Democrats holding majorities in the House and Senate. His response, in essence, was that this was one of the rare times when no strong domestic policy leadership could be found at either end of Pennsylvania Avenue. Bush was not much engaged in domestic issues, he said; Speaker

Tom Foley and Majority Leader George Mitchell were nice men, but neither had a real agenda for the country.

I thought that less than persuasive, and apparently so did the country's voters. In 1992, they chose unified government for the first time in a dozen years. But the fiasco of Bill Clinton's first two years, climaxed with the collapse of his ambitious national health care plan in a Democratic Congress, produced a massive midterm election swing to the GOP. In 1994, for the first time in forty years, Republicans gained control of both the House and the Senate.

The first year of that divided government produced gridlock of the worst kind, including an impasse on the budget that forced two shutdowns of government. The Republicans faced the same kind of public revulsion that Democrats had encountered a year earlier. Being smart politicians, they decided to mend their ways. Clinton made it easy for them by following the advice of his new political guru Dick Morris to "triangulate" himself away from congressional Democrats and strike a more conservative stance on the budget and other issues.

It is at that point that De Vries and Tarrance begin their narrative. They point out that in 1996, Clinton and the Republican Congress were able to agree on a series of domestic measures, raising the minimum wage, making health insurance more accessible, and, most significant, turning the welfare system over to the states. The cooperative relationship was endorsed by the voters in the 1996 election, which made Clinton the first re-elected Democratic president since FDR and also made Newt Gingrich, his sometimes nemesis, the first Republican since Nicholas Longworth in the 1920s to serve consecutive terms as Speaker.

The reluctant partnership produced an even bigger achievement in 1997, when the White House and Congress forged an agreement that promised a balanced budget by 2002 at the latest. A booming economy moved that achievement forward by three years, and both Congress and Clinton in early 1998 enjoyed the highest approval scores they had seen in years. "Competitive cooperation," the authors assert, has finally come into its own.

Their final argument is that public support for this arrangement is likely to continue to grow. That support is fed by two separate sources and comes from separate voter coalitions. In a time of widespread distrust of government, many voters believe that dividing power enables the parties to keep an eye on each other and stop imprudent actions before they start. Others who take a more positive view of government say that divided control produces fuller policy debate, more balanced and innovative solutions, and a better-informed public.

Correctly or not, many in both camps say they see this new pattern of divided government as fulfilling the Constitution writers' belief in the separation of powers and the system of checks and balances.

"In effect," the authors write, "America is entering a new era of coalition government," one that will emphasize fiscal discipline, smaller budgets and bureaucracies, and more devolution of responsibility to the states.

This is a bold — but not implausible — scenario. Whether it actually develops depends on many factors. A major scandal in the Democratic administration or a sharp reversal of the good economic news of the last five years could drastically reduce Democratic chances of holding the White House. An attractive, charismatic candidate — a new Ronald Reagan — could give the Republicans a presidential winner as soon as 2000.

Less plausibly, Newt Gingrich and Trent Lott could make such serious tactical mistakes in opposing popular legislation or backing distasteful measures that Democrats could regain their old majorities in the House and Senate. This is the least likely scenario, because powerful demographic trends — the shift of population to the South and West — are expanding the number of House seats where Republicans are favored while reducing the size of the Democrats' base in the old cities of the Northeast and Midwest.

For all these reasons, we are, in my judgment, likelier to see the White House switch to the Republicans than Congress revert to Democratic control. But we have no idea at this point whether the country would react favorably or critically to unified Republican government. We have not seen such a government since Eisenhower was first elected. The power centers in the GOP and the controlling ideology are far different now than they were then.

It is quite possible that Republicans would blow the opportunity as swiftly and completely as the Democrats did under Clinton in 1993–94. But one should remember that the Democratic fiasco of those years was not foreordained. Suppose Clinton had accepted the urgings of some strategists and attempted welfare reform, not health care reform, in the 103rd Congress. With a modicum of luck, he could have assembled a remarkable record in his first two years.

It would have started with three big measures that actually did pass: a major deficit-reduction bill that boosted the economy and moved the budget toward balance; a major crime bill that accelerated the decline in lawbreaking, especially in major cities; and a major trade bill creating the North American Free Trade zone. In addition, Clinton and the Democrats might have had a minimum-wage increase (which was postponed only because all employers were being asked to shoulder health insurance premiums for their workers), and a major welfare-reform bill.

With a record like that, Democrats might well have gotten through the 1994 election with only the minor dip in their majorities that the parties of most newly elected presidents have experienced. Certainly there would have been much in the record for liberals, moderates, and conservatives to embrace — as we learned when Clinton and Congress actually followed this course in 1996 and 1997.

But all this is surmise. The reading of history and of the polls that Tarrance and De Vries offer is certainly a plausible one. And it comes from scholars who have been right far more often than they have been wrong in gauging the pattern of American politics.

So read on and decide for yourself.

DAVID S. BRODER
The Washington Post

Acknowledgments

Acknowledging those who have contributed to this work is a difficult task because so many have contributed to our professional development in many ways. We extend our appreciation to all those who will recognize their efforts throughout this book.

In particular, Everett Ladd of The Roper Center needs to be thanked for his contribution in the *Public Perspective* magazine for highlighting the powerful confirming evidence of divided government. This consolidating research essentially served as a guidepost for many of the ideas in the book.

Inspiration was given by Morris Fiorina of Harvard University, who with David Mayhew of Yale University laid the groundwork on divided government, so that we might link divided government with ticket-splitting. Fiorina, in reading the manuscript, provided us encouragement and timely observations.

No one should be thanked more strenuously than the professionals of The Gallup Poll at The Gallup Organization in Princeton, New Jersey. Frank Newport, editor-in-chief, and Lydia Saad, managing editor, were instrumental in opening up the opportunity to this original research and updating the ticket-splitting trends so the book could contain the latest possible data on this phenomenon. Many of the more recent Gallup polls were conducted for CNN/USA Today, and we thank them for making their data available to the public.

Tom Mann of the Brookings Institution, Bill Connelly of Washington and Lee University, Thad Beyle of the University of North Carolina, and Rhodes Cook, former senior political writer of the

Congressional Quarterly, patiently read evolving versions of the manuscript, offering valuable critique and insight. Their informal con-
versations and questions broadened the depth of our research and
scholarship. Karlynn Bowman of the American Enterprise Institute
facilitated the publication of the manuscript as she recognized the
value of this research to the political science discipline.

We thank David S. Broder of *The Washington Post* for taking time
from his very busy schedule to read the manscript and write the
foreword. And we're grateful to John N. Davis for his witty and
insightful addition of the case study in North Carolina.

Ken Rietz, Stacey Hudson, and Heather Overstreet of Burson-
Marsteller, Washington, D.C., and Clair Holt and Barbara Johnson
of the North Carolina Institute of Political Leadership have also
supported the production of this book.

Serving as editor and researcher, Donna Mosher cannot be held
responsible for what we had to say about the complexities of American politics in the 1990s. But she deserves significant credit for
making our observations understandable. Her ability to synthesize
the perspectives from the co-authors' combined decades of political
experience and voting research, as well as her willingness to conduct
the original interviews of respondents across the nation, allowed us
to complete this book. She coined the phrase "competitive cooperation," allowing us to introduce the concept to political science. As
the researcher, she served as the link between our thinking and that
of the 30 Gallup Poll respondents with whom she spoke.

Without those 30 respondents, however, this book would not
exist. They essentially served as a "national focus group," providing
insights that until now have not been chronicled in such detail. In
sharing their candid thoughts and opinions, each of them has made
an immeasurable contribution to our efforts and to the field of
political science. We thank them.

LANCE TARRANCE
WALT DE VRIES

CHAPTER ONE

The New Era of Competitive Cooperation

Part I: The Evolution of Modern Coalition Government

WASHINGTON, July 23, 1996 — Clinton Signs Welfare Bill Amid Division

Clinton signed historic welfare legislation yesterday that re-writes six decades of social policy, ending the federal guarantee of cash assistance to the poor and turning welfare programs over to the states.

Whatever divisiveness it has inspired, the bill's enactment is likely to be remembered as a defining moment for Clinton.

"The two parties cannot attack each other over it," Clinton said. "Politicians cannot attack poor people over it. . . . This is not the end of welfare reform, this is the beginning. And we all have to assume responsibility."

Washington Post

WASHINGTON, July 29, 1997 — Clinton, Congress OK Budget Deal

The White House and GOP leaders last night announced a tentative agreement on the final details of a long-sought, five-year

1

plan to balance the budget, revamp the Medicare program and provide the first major tax cut since the early 1980s.

President Clinton and Republican leaders both claimed important political victories on tax and spending policies in the plan, with Clinton earlier saying it could be "the achievement of a generation."

Perhaps the most remarkable thing to be said about the balanced budget and tax cut package as outlined by congressional Republicans yesterday was how little sacrifice it appeared to require from either side.

Washington Post

WASHINGTON, August 1, 1997 — Americans bless Clinton and congressional Republicans for cooperating

Congress gets its highest public approval since Republicans took over. In a new Wall Street Journal/NBC News poll, 48% approve of the job lawmakers are doing. By a six-point margin, Americans are more inclined to say they want next year's election to produce a Republican Congress. But Clinton's job approval also stays high at 56%, and for his handling of the economy he gets his highest marks ever.

Just over half say the president and Congress are working well together.

Wall Street Journal

Politics as usual it isn't.

In a matter of months between 1996 and 1997, the United States Congress brokered legislation that increased the minimum wage, reformed welfare, made health insurance more portable, and — most significantly — promised to balance the budget within five years. A chemical weapons treaty was ratified, resetting the Consumer Price Index was placed on the bargaining table, and talk was even raised regarding saving Medicare and revamping the Social Security system.

Reluctant cooperation between Capitol Hill and the White House has reached a hallmark unseen along Pennsylvania Avenue since the inauguration of Dwight Eisenhower. It has come with a share of cumbersome growing pains, but is resulting in effective legislation and, most significantly, a fundamental change in American politics.

2

"We have divided government, and I think it is good," said Sam Donaldson. "The political parties are so evenly balanced" (ABC News, June 15, 1997).

The Power Struggle

Americans are seeing the emergence of an era of competitive cooperation, distilled from a heady dose of failure. From 1993 through 1997, both parties struggled to grasp singular control of the power, and both experienced traumatic defeats in the eyes of the American public.

In 1993, Clinton began this disruptive and perplexing four-year period counting on the traditional support of a Democratic Congress. Striving a week into his presidency to make good on a political campaign debt, rather he found himself alienating a significant portion of the electorate as he attempted to redefine the position of gays in the military. His proposed "don't ask, don't tell" policy was met with skepticism and outright derision among voters, political leaders, and the media.

Democratic Senator Sam Nunn, the Armed Services Committee chairman, opposed lifting the ban and urged Clinton to exercise restraint in taking decisive action. Massachusetts Representative Barney Frank tried to brighten the scenario, supposing that Democratic members compelled to vote against Clinton's pledge to allow gays in the military would feel more compelled to support Clinton on his economic issues. But perhaps the greatest impact the White House felt was from the American voters, who placed more than 400,000 phone calls the day before the announcement was expected, more than ten times the normal volume (*Chicago Tribune*, 1/28/93, p. 1).

Clinton subsequently experienced another significant and enormous setback in the failure of his health-care-reform effort, despite the fact that he had a Democratic Congress to back him up. When Clinton in October 1993 proposed health insurance coverage for all before a joint session of Congress, nearly 60 percent of Americans supported some sort of universal healthcare coverage.

But by the following July, the polls showed a mere 40 percent supporting the Clinton initiative mandating a top-heavy undertak-

3

ing requiring thousands of new bureaucrats at the cost of tax dollars and jobs in the private sector. Senate Majority Leader George Mitchell of Maine, charged with ushering the measure through Congress to the Oval Office for signature, in September 1994 acquiesced to the dwindling pulse of public opinion and conceded failure. The effort to make the sweeping changes introduced so optimistically by the Clintons during the honeymoon phase of their presidency was dead by October 1994 (*USA Today*, 9/27/94, p. 8A; *USA Today*, 10/5/94, p. 10A).

This struck a real blow to the concept that reform and change are possible only in a context of one-party control with accountability at the polls. And observers of American politics were beginning to glimpse an emerging influence of public opinion on legislation between elections.

The political tables were turned a year later when the Republicans took control of the House after the 1994 elections. Led by newly elected House Speaker Newt Gingrich, the Congress twice experienced setbacks when they could not reach a budget consensus with the White House. In November 1995, while awaiting a consensus in budget negotiations between the two branches, the federal government was forced to shut down many of its operations. Once again, the American public reacted with revulsion to such tactics, with a Washington Post–ABC News poll reporting 71 percent of Americans — including a majority of Republicans — disapproving of the way the Republicans handled the dispute (*Washington Post*, 11/21/95, p. A4).

A low point of public confidence in American government was reached the second time the Gingrich-led GOP sent home federal employees. Few Americans saw anything positive resulting from the impasse. Voters expressed a concern with politicians being incapable of solving big problems confronting the country and seemed convinced that both Clinton and congressional Republicans were more interested in gaining partisan leverage than reaching fiscal compromise for the public good.

The New Era Begins as the
1996 Presidential Campaign Unfolds

Early 1996 brought the awakening of Congress to the public's insistence that the federal government begin to respond to demands for effective legislation in a framework of fiscal responsibility.

The first evidence of a new atmosphere of bipartisan cooperation was in the passing of the line-item veto, in which the Republican-controlled House was committed enough to the issue that they were even willing to give the veto to a Democratic president. Initiated by Ronald Reagan twelve years earlier, the legislation had a monumental effect, noted in April on the editorial page of the *Wall Street Journal:*

> What's extraordinary, and praiseworthy, now is that a Republican Congress has voted to hand this power to a Democratic president. . . . The veto never would have passed if Tom Foley were still Speaker of the House. . . . When even liberal Democrats feel obliged to support the item veto, you know where the tide of history is moving.
>
> Twelve years seem like a long time from proposal to passage, but in the difficult American system it often takes that long to break the back of business as usual.
>
> *Wall Street Journal,* 4/1/96, p. A14

This step paved the way for further significant cooperation between the parties, including three high-profile pieces of legislation signed into law by President Clinton within three days.

On August 20, 1996, in a ceremony on the south lawn of the White House, the Marine Corps band heralded a clear Democratic victory as Clinton signed into law an increase in the federal minimum wage. When this legislation was first introduced, its prospects for passage in the Republican-controlled Congress were viewed as dim. But with the jelling of a new sense of bipartisan cooperation, the bill passed by wide margins in both houses.

The next day, Clinton signed the Kennedy-Kassebaum bill, permitting workers to take their health insurance from job to job. Perhaps more significant than the legislation itself was the linking of liberal Massachusetts Senator Ted Kennedy with bulwark Republican Nancy Landon Kassebaum (*Washington Post,* 8/21/96).

The cornerstone of competitive cooperation was set on August 22, 1996, as President Clinton ended sixty years of social welfare policy, signing into law the Personal Responsibility and Work Opportunity Reconciliation Act of 1996. The welfare reform act transferred the responsibility from the federal government over to the states, required recipients to work, and limited benefits to five years.

Once again, the significance of the legislation lay in the process as much as the results. The bipartisan political support leading to the reform was noted by Clinton as he stressed the importance of removing welfare from the political arena. "The two parties cannot attack each other over it. . . . We all have to assume responsibility" (*Washington Post*, 7/23/96).

The public overwhelmingly supported the bipartisan cooperation rarely seen between the two competing political parties. The Gallup Organization found, in a poll taken during the negotiations on Capitol Hill, that 68 percent of respondents approved the congressional action on welfare reform, with 15 percent opposed to the change. Rarely has congressional action seen such an endorsement by a normally skeptical public (CNN/*USA Today*/Gallup Poll, August 5–7, 1996).

Nearly two years later, the public was validated as Clinton and the Congress wrestled for credit on the success of the new welfare policy.

Administration and congressional studies show that the welfare caseloads nationally have dropped dramatically, prompting an election-year scramble among Democrats and Republicans eager to claim credit for the smallest benefit rolls since 1969.

At the White House on Wednesday President Clinton touted the success of the Welfare to Work Partnership . . . and the 1996 welfare reform law as contributing factors that have helped states move more than 3.3 million recipients off the rolls and into jobs since 1994.

While Clinton was singing the praises of welfare reform, Republicans were trying to claim some credit for helping to change the face of the benefit system that they say has given as much help to the lazy as it has to the poor and unfortunate. . . . House Ways and Means Comitteee Chairman Bill Archer gave the Republican-controlled Congress and the states equal credit for implementing the kind of reforms that he said emphasize the importance of work over government "handouts." . . .

"We've changed the welfare state into an opportunity society, and we can all be proud of this great achievement," added Archer, a key player in the 1996 overhaul of the federal welfare system.

Houston Chronicle, 5/28/98

1996 Election Mandate of Shared Power

These successes were affirmed by voters in the 1996 elections as they returned to Washington a Democratic president and a Republican-controlled Congress, paving the way for more legislative accomplishments carved from competitive cooperation, albeit reluctantly.

The welfare reform bill was a major force in the 1996 election results because it exhibited a historic breakthrough on a major policy issue that had concerned Americans for three decades, proving that competitive cooperation could work. Shortly after Clinton signed the bill, Gallup polled Americans for their reflections on the Republican Congress working with a Democratic president. Both were deemed by respondents to be working successfully. Thus, success by both parties was not mutually exclusive. Gridlock was no longer to be taken for granted as a given result of divided party control of the government. The Gallup polls during this election cycle proved the point:

''Since the start of 1995 when Republicans took control of Congress, in general, would you say the Republican Congress has been a success or a failure?''

	May 1996	August 1996	Political change
Success	43%	48%	+5%
Failure	49	43	-6

''Looking back at Bill Clinton's first term in office, in general, would you say his presidency has been a success or a failure?''

	Dec. 1994	August 1996	Political change
Success	44%	64%	+20%
Failure	50	31	-19

The Gallup Organization

7

These data, in retrospect, were some of the most important leading indicators that voters were willing to reaffirm the new status quo, but only after testing the parties on welfare reform and their willingness to cooperate even under intense competition. As voters approached the 1998 mid-term Congressional elections, their support of the GOP-controlled Congress was even more positive. The Gallup Poll taken in April 1998 showed the "success" responses had reached a level of 58 percent, more than 10 points up from the previous election cycle.

New Control of the U.S. Congress

"Since the start of 1995 when Republicans took control of Congress, in general, would you say the Republican Congress has been a success or a failure?"

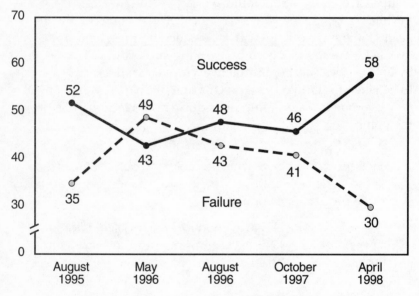

Source: The Gallup Organization

President Bill Clinton won re-election in 1996 by a comfortable electoral college margin over Republican Bob Dole, but with less than a majority of the voters. He was unable to fulfill historical precedents to lead the Democrats to majorities in the House and the Senate. Rather, Clinton became the first Democratic president in history elected with a House and Senate controlled by the opposition.

The Republicans were unable to win the 67 Senate seats to overturn a presidential veto, or even the 60 needed to defeat a Democratic filibuster, and even lost seats in the House, dropping from 235 seats to 227.

Overall, the balance of power between the two political parties lent but a nominal edge to the House Republicans, with a Congressional electoral vote giving Republicans 49.0 percent to 48.5 percent for the Democrats, a true balance of power at this level.

Interestingly enough, this *realpolitik* was grasped in the final weeks of the election by the National Republican Congressional Committee, as evidenced in the "Crystal Ball" television commercial, run with borrowed money just days before the election. In a last-minute effort to salvage Republican control of the Congress while tacitly acknowledging the futility of a Dole presidential victory, the campaign committee invested funds in a subtle admission that divided control of Washington was better than no control at all.

''What would happen if the Democrats controlled Congress and the White House? Been there, done that. Remember? The largest tax increase in history, more wasteful Washington spending, a government-run health care scheme. The liberal special interests aligned with Clinton, desperately want to buy back control of Congress. If we give the special interests a blank check in Congress, who's going to represent us?''

This was a defining moment in the 1996 elections, with the congressional wing of the Republican party asking voters to return Republican members of Congress to work with a Democrat.

A post-election poll by the *Los Angeles Times* asked, "Are you happy or unhappy that the Republican Party maintained control of the U.S. Congress?" It is interesting to note the number of non-

Republicans who supported the new status quo — 69 percent of the Perot voters and 65 percent of the independents.

	Happy	Unhappy	Don't Know
Total	65%	27%	8%
Independents	65	23	12
Clinton voters	39	49	12
Perot voters	69	19	12

Los Angeles Times, November 5, 1996

The Aftermath in 1997

Less than six months into 1997, the 105th Congress continued strides toward legislative efficacy with cooperation between the White House and Senate in executive branch appointments, including Republican Bill Cohen as secretary of defense.

In late April, the Senate approved a global treaty banning the production and use of chemical weapons. This hard-won major foreign policy victory for Clinton was the result of the support of Senate Majority Leader Trent Lott, who swayed the votes of more than a dozen key Republicans, delivering seven more votes than the required two-thirds majority for the ratification of treaties. A surprising endorsement by former presidential candidate Bob Dole contributed to the strength of the ratification.

"This vote is an example of America working as it should, Democrats and Republicans working together, putting our country first, reaching across party lines, reaching for the common good," Clinton said. "This vote is vivid proof that we are stronger as a nation when we work together." (*Washington Post*, 4/25/97, p. 1) This comment reflects a marked contrast from 1993, when Clinton won passage of a tax increase without a single GOP vote and passage was gained only with a vice-presidential tie-breaking vote.

Capping the legislative accomplishments altering the political panorama was the landmark balanced budget agreement of 1997, promising to eliminate the federal deficit within five years and balance the budget for the first time since 1969.

The budget compromise gave Clinton the educational tax credits he sought, the full $24 billion he requested for children's health care, and a $500-per-child tax credit extended to parents in low-wage jobs who pay little or no income tax. The president also won an increase in the cigarette tax.

The Republicans landed huge cuts in the capital gains and estate taxes, in addition to the commitment to a balanced budget, all long-standing party goals.

The 1997 balanced budget agreement is arguably the most significant piece of legislation to bear a presidential imprimatur since the last time it was achieved — in 1969. And the speed with which the agreement was reached was unprecedented, fueled by a boisterous economy and an optimistic outlook for the future. And the congressional Republicans finally began to regain support from the public, as they evolved from their traditional static posture that brought about the "Contract with America," moving into a new era of competitive cooperation.

A nationwide Gallup Poll conducted in August 1997 lends insight to the public interpretations of this historic precedent:

``As you may know, the Republican leaders in Congress recently passed and President Clinton signed a federal budget plan which makes changes in taxes and spending which they say will balance the federal budget by the year 2002. Who do you think is more responsible for this federal budget plan, President Clinton or the Republican leaders in Congress?''

    31% President Clinton
    51   The Republican leaders in Congress
    11   Both equally
     2   Neither/other
     5   No opinion

                                    The Gallup Organization

Part II: The New Politics of Coalition Government

INDIANAPOLIS, Aug. 22, 1997 — Gingrich Offers Upbeat View

Just hours after House Speaker Newt Gingrich attempted to reassure nervous Republicans that GOP leaders remain committed to the conservative agenda, former vice president Dan Quayle . . . suggested the Republican congressional leadership sold out to President Clinton in the recently enacted agreement to trim taxes and balance the budget by 2002.

Quayle scornfully suggested that the GOP's "Contract with America" has become "the contract with Clinton."

Washington Post

EDGARTOWN, Mass. — Sept. 7, 1997

Al From, director of the Democratic Leadership Council, the centrist organization Clinton helped found in the 1980s, maintains the president already has a place in history by helping shift the Democratic Party's policies toward the middle and giving rise to an activist, yet fiscally restrained, government.

"How can you say reversing three decades of deficits is small-bore?" He cited the balanced budget plan and the end of welfare guarantees as historic accomplishments.

Houston Chronicle

What makes these legislative victories significant is the fact that they have been crafted by a Republican-controlled Congress and signed into law by a Democratic president. Yet this is not the first time over the last three decades the American people have expected the two political parties to share the control. What makes the 105th Congress different from the previous Congresses controlled by a different majority party than the party in the White House? What is making divided government work in the 1990s, with a Democratic president and a Republican Congress, when it produced little more than political gridlock in the 1980s, when the Republicans controlled the White House and the Democrats ran the Congress?

It is this slim, even fragile, balance of power between the executive and legislative branches of government that has forced a consensus and crafted the legislative accomplishments of 1997. The political scales have essentially been counterweighted to an extent not seen in generations. The American electorate has installed in Washington, D.C., a Democratic president — with less than a majority vote of its citizens — and a Congress that, while it is controlled by the Republicans, remains closely balanced between the two parties.

Moreover, the last decade of peace and prosperity has asked little of the American citizens in terms of supporting a dominant international position or endorsing sweeping economic programs to alleviate financial strife. Rather than the politicians shaping the public panorama, the 1990s has seen the American electorate again training its eye on, and increasing its expectations of, the politicians. This demand for efficacy, particularly from the millions of Perot voters, has forced the government to embark on a winning, albeit rocky, road to political and policy reform.

Third-party presidential candidate Ross Perot's contribution to transforming the political discourse should be noted as well, and applauded. Perot's candidacy, while unsuccessful electorally, was exceedingly instrumental in redirecting the national debate and training the public eye on the issues of the federal deficit and fiscal responsibility. It is important to note that 20 million voters in 1992 rejected both major political party candidates, voting for a third-party candidate. Four years later, even though a vote for him would register for little more than a protest, Perot had forced both parties to acknowledge his agenda as he garnered the support of 10 million voters, still a substantial bloc of Americans who continued to reject both major parties, while voting for a new status quo for the future.

Conclusion

Thus, the American people shaped public policy by placing demands on the two parties to cooperate in ways that each might consider contrary to their overall benefit. The parties are responding, reluctantly, to the demands of the electorate; and the results achieved come from compromise born from healthy political competition.

In fact, should the old balance of power have been reinstated in 1996 in favor of one party, these policy successes would never have been achieved. The Democrats most assuredly would not have voted to balance the budget or reduce taxes. The Republicans would have attempted to balance the budget, but not with the increases in spending allocated to education and the environment.

Thus, shared control has generated real, albeit reluctant, progress for both parties. The Democrats were able to win spending increases, thereby continuing their image as the compassionate party, while the Republicans were able to validate their position as the party dedicated to fiscal discipline and lower taxes. Few, if any, political commentators would have predicted such developments; and, indeed, this evolution of efficacy has not been understood by many political scientists and other observers whose analyses have used the traditional models of unified political accountability.

The Gallup Poll in September 1997 asked a question that defines today's new era, demonstrating a dramatic increase (+14%) in support for divided control:

''Do you think it is better for the country to have a President who comes from the same political party that controls Congress, or do you think it is better to have a President from one political party and Congress controlled by another?''

	September 1992	October 1994	September 1997
Same party	47%	45%	31%
Different parties	31	37	45
No difference/No opinion	22	18	24

Ongoing polling by Gallup showed the support for divided government dropping somewhat, but still maintaining a plurality over the support for unified control. This could be attributed largely to the commencement of the 1998 campaigns and increasing public awareness of political issues.

Divided Government Trend
1992-1998

''Do you think it is better for the country to have a president who comes from the same political party that controls Congress, or from one political party and Congress controlled by another?''

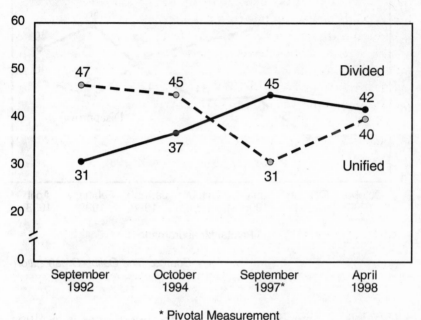

* Pivotal Measurement

Source: The Gallup Organization

U.S. Congress Approval Trend
1990-1998

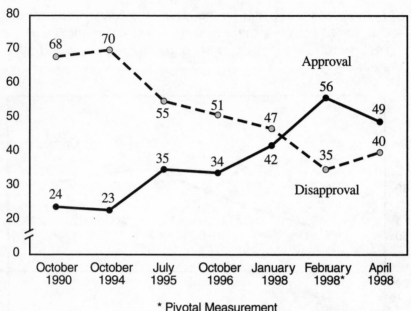

* Pivotal Measurement

Source: The Gallup Organization

This delicate shared power between the two parties is resulting in a forced cooperation, or reluctant consensus, between the executive branch and the legislative branch. Based on party competitiveness, for the first time in this century both parties are extremely well balanced, and neither can afford not to cooperate with the other. The alternatives to this forced cooperation are stalemate, or gridlock, which the American electorate made clear is not acceptable at this time, and one-party control, which the voters believe leads to excessive domination and centralization, which run counter to current societal themes of decentralization and devolution. As voters now look at what has happened, a plurality think "it is better to have a President from one political party and Congress controlled by another."

U.S. Climate of Satisfaction

''In general, are you satisfied or dissatisfied with the way things are going in the United States at this time?''

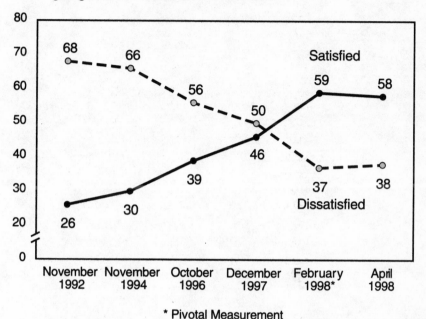

* Pivotal Measurement

Source: The Gallup Organization

WASHINGTON, November 12, 1997

Polls show Americans are fairly satisfied with the way the Republican Congress and Democratic White House have worked together on the federal budget and taxes. There seems little desire to return to one-party rule. And the Republican sweep of the off-year elections this month (Nov. 1997) doesn't bode well for Democrats or the Reform Party in 1998.

USA Today

CHAPTER TWO

Do Voters Choose Divided Government?

Divided government is not new to our experience as a nation, but there are some respects in which the contemporary era is unique. . . . To some degree, divided government in the United States probably reflects a lack of popular consensus about important issues and a consequent unwillingness to trust either party with the full power to govern.

Morris Fiorina, *Divided Government*, 1996

One of the questions being asked after the 1996 presidential election was whether a critical portion of the electorate deliberately voted *for* divided government. The question ought to be reframed into three parts: do voters prefer continued political party confrontations and stalemate; do voters prefer a blank-check policy for either parties; or, as in our current context, do voters now prefer competitive cooperation between evenly balanced political parties? Academics and political elites have traditionally assumed that divided government will always lead to inefficient government and ineffective policies, seeing "little beyond drift and stalemate in a divided political system." Woodrow Wilson, a strong proponent of this elitist view, once succinctly summarized the traditional "responsible-party" model of unified party control when he

19

said, "You cannot compound a successful government out of antagonisms."

Current political research is discovering a new model of coalition government, in which some voters consciously have been making their individual voting decisions with divided government *an intentional choice*. The following conclusion was made in the post-election report on the 1996 elections by the Gallup Organization:

> In the final days before the election, with Clinton's victory seemingly a foregone conclusion, many Republican congressional candidates campaigned on the theme that the country needed a "balance" to President Clinton, and that a return of the Democratic Congress would bring with it a return to big government. A post-election Gallup poll suggests this last-minute strategy may have been the final key to the narrow Republican victory in the House.

Further research clearly shows that the public certainly is not unhappy with shared control, despite many of the scholarly criticisms of a government that is operating under divided control.

A leading authority on divided government, Morris Fiorina of Harvard University, writes:

> At this time in our history, the American electorate typically chooses to split control of our governing institutions between the parties. Why? That is the question that has been of most concern to academics. . . . Only if we understand how we have gotten to where we are can we predict where we will go if we tinker with our institutions and political processes. To put it more colloquially, if we fail to understand why divided government has come to be, we will have no one to blame if well-meaning reforms throw us out of the divided government frying pan into the unified government fire.

What the Voters Are Saying

Special in-depth interviews (IDIs) conducted with respondents to 1996 Gallup post-election polls provide even deeper insights into the new mind-set of the ticket-splitters of the 1990s.

In-depth interviews were conducted with Gallup poll respondents who voted for the president of one political party and chose their U.S. representative from another party. Respondents were first asked if they felt such a division of power is good. The overwhelming approval for divided government was evident, with the desire for increased checks and balances a common theme running throughout the responses.

Respondents to the extended interviews were asked the following question: *"Many people today say that the voters in the United States live in an era or time of 'divided government'; or 'split control' — that is, when one political party is elected to the White House as President and a different political party is elected to the majority in the U.S. Congress. Some believe that this division of power is a good thing, while others do not. What do you think?"*

In-Depth Interviews with
Clinton-Republican Ticket-Splitters

It was found in the IDIs that Clinton-Republican ticket-splitters — those who voted for Clinton for president and for their Republican House candidate — shared many supportive views of divided government. They say they were trying to maintain the new status quo, the current balance of power. They wanted to assure that diverse opinions are heard and that more of a public forum is created to discuss issues. These respondents exhibit a rational response to the world today. They consider checks and balances of the political parties a useful policy tool, without wild swings from one political approach to the next. Here are their own words:

"I'd say it's a good thing," responded a 64-year-old grandfather from New Jersey who voted for Clinton and is retired, but works part time selling real estate. "I think it keeps one group from getting so strong that they run everything their way; then there's no checks and balances."

"I think it depends upon the election," said Elizabeth, 31, who felt the Republicans did not offer a viable presidential candidate. "When you're not happy with either party, [shared control is] probably a good bet."

21

Irene, 86, lives in Arizona, considers herself a Democrat and voted for Clinton, but refuses to vote for a candidate on party affiliation. "Well, based on the way I voted, I think I voted that way because I felt the Republican running for Congress was the superior person, and I want the best people in Congress, not necessarily whether they are Republicans or Democrats."

An Indiana university administrator said he would prefer more unanimity between the two branches of government, but appreciated the different views that could be presented with shared control. "I see advantages and disadvantages, honestly. Disadvantages are the roadblocks that seem to come along. The advantages are the checks and balances; that we don't take wild swings one way or the other."

"I think it's a good thing," said a 74-year-old man from North Carolina who voted for Clinton. "If you have a Democrat majority, with a Democrat president, they do just whatever they want to. Pass any legislation they want. It makes no difference. With the two parties in, they have to compromise and keep things on the level."

Marshall, a 31-year-old father in Ohio, considers himself a Republican but was not willing to abandon Clinton for what he saw as uncertainty in Bob Dole. He said he saw shared control resulting in a more aggressive government and better legislation. "There are pros and cons to anything that goes through. I think if you have split control, it's more apt to bring out some of the controversy for closer examination."

"Basically, each party can keep a check on the other party," said David, 36, who voted for Clinton because he saw him moderating his positions in four years. "I think it's a good idea because they're either too liberal or too conservative, and this way it kind of evens them out."

In-Depth Interviews with Perot-Republican Ticket-Splitters

Perot-Republican ticket-splitters — supporting Perot for president and Republican House candidates — were found to be especially supportive of divided government, expressing a desire for a stronger "watchdog" effect on government. These IDIs clearly communicated the typical "outsider" antipathy toward government. These respondents stressed most strongly the need for checks and balances, often volunteering the desire for such control before the issue was raised in the next question. Here is how they responded:

"I think it CAN be a good thing," said 39-year-old Vince, a cabinet maker from New Jersey. He voted for Perot because he felt Perot would make tough choices necessary for the best interest of the country. "It gives a check and balance. If you have people who totally agree all the time on everything they do, then they become close-minded."

Darlene, 66, from Illinois, voted for Perot and supported an increased scrutiny of the legislative process. "My main feeling is it doesn't make any difference as long as the people you send are good people. I don't think it should make any difference party-wise. If you have a president of one party, and the Congress of the other, at least it's a checkmate."

"It's a good thing," said Paul, 38, a salesman and father of three from New York. "It provides checks and balances. It gets two agendas from two parties, and there's more of a reason for compromise, and things to get through; otherwise, if they can't work together, nothing gets passed."

"I like Democrats generally more for domestic policy and Republicans for foreign policy. With the mix of the two it makes for a good balance," replied a 24-year-old Perot voter and advertising copywriter from Minneapolis.

A 33-year-old single woman from Michigan said she thought divided government increased checks and balances. "I think a lot of people are voting for individuals, for people they have personal contact with, or somebody they know or have followed for a time. They know that person based on their integrity. They're more apt to vote for that person rather than along party lines. Traditionally, in my understanding, [our political system] was set up to balance power, and I think that's a good thing. One-party control is almost anti-American."

"I think it [divided government] is a good thing, because the parties can keep a check on each other," said a 54-year-old Hispanic woman from west Texas who voted for Perot. "Everybody needs to be checked on sometimes."

"I don't really see a good or a bad point to it," said Jack, a

50-year-old truck driver from Oklahoma who voted for Perot. He used to consider himself a Democrat, but now sees himself simply as an American. "Sometimes when you get the old-line party out, it kind of wakes them up and lets them know they're not invincible. I think it's good the Republicans are in control of the Congress right now. The Democrats have become so corrupt and so free-spending they were leading the nation to bankruptcy."

The New Mind-Set for the Next Generation of Voters?

The IDIs in our research revealed a new mind-set in the way the American electorate wants the political power distributed in Washington. They attempted to define the terms "separation of powers" and "checks and balances," correlating them to the function of the political parties rather than the strict institutional relationship of power between the branches of government.

Voters who said they intentionally voted for divided government were asked by the Gallup Organization in their post-election survey after the 1996 elections whether they deliberately tried to split their votes for institutional reasons, rather than candidate reasons. Gallup queried only those voters who voted for Clinton and a Republican House candidate (7%), whose votes reflected the general outcome of the election, and those who voted for Dole and Democratic House candidates (3%), whose votes were contrary to the outcome.

''Which is the main reason why you supported the Republican/Democratic candidate in your district?''

	Clinton-Republicans	Dole-Democrats
Because you thought he or she was the best candidate:	75%	82%
Because you wanted to provide balance to your vote:	16	1
Neither/Other	8	15

The Gallup Organization
(1996 post-election)

24

From a purely quantitative standpoint, the results might seem less than spectacular, in that one-sixth of the Clinton-Republican ticket-splitters said they were deliberately trying to balance the power in Washington, D.C. However, the Gallup Organization, in their post-election summary, notes the significance of this percentage: "One in six voters who voted for a Republican after having voted for Clinton said they did so to provide 'balance' to their Clinton vote. While the number of such party switchers is small, the *net effect would have been more than enough to provide the GOP its margin of victory.*" (*The 1996 Election, Americans Stay the Course,* by Newport, Saad, and Moore, Gallup, December 1996; emphasis added)

Virtually none of the Dole-Democrat ticket-splitters chose the balancing choice to the question, and thus we're left with the idea that approximately, at best, only 2 percent of the voters were trying to strategically balance the power between the two parties and the two branches of government. Voters were very traditional in their responses, saying they were voting for the best candidate, but our post-election in-depth interviews revealed that they were indeed very happy — in hindsight — with what they had done.

Ticket-splitters thus have become the fulcrum of the new balance of power in American politics today. And while the approximately 80 percent of the United States voters who were straight-ticket Republicans (voting for Republicans for president and representative) and straight-ticket Democrats (voting for Democrats for president and representative) may not feel very comfortable with these results, our research shows that divided government is here to stay.

The Debate over Democratic Theory

If the ticket-splitters are so comfortable with divided government, as perhaps a personal choice and also their preference for a more competitive political marketplace, then why are so many academics and political elites against divided government?

David Mayhew of Yale University cited several critics of divided government in his 1991 book *Divided We Govern:*

Political scientist Randall Ripley argued in 1969 that "to have a productive majority in the American system of government, the president and the majority of both houses must be from the *same* party. Such a condition does not guarantee legislative success, but is necessary for it." V. O. Key, Jr., wrote "Common partisan control of the executive and the legislature does not assure energetic government, but division of party control precludes it." . . . Lloyd Cutler concluded in a piece attacking divided control: ". . . there has never been in modern days any successful domestic legislative program in a time of divided government."

This prevailing view among "unified government" academics would be best summarized by historian James McGregor Burns, who, in a 1989 interview with journalist Bill Moyers, suggested that America might be the "worst-managed of all the great Western countries." In his view, the constitutional system that purposely separates power fragments government, frustrates centralization and issue cohesion, and makes it impossible to give the country effective leadership in the long run. Burns went on to say that

> the original framers of our Constitution were so concerned about oppressive government that the way they tamed the beast was to divide power very carefully among the President and the Senate and the House, and the judiciary, down to the state level, and the local level, very carefully, allotting Constitutional power to different parts of the government with different constituencies. . . . So Madison, Hamilton and Jefferson arranged a system that would check-mate power and deadlock it. . . . And the sad thing is that the political parties have declined so that one of the great unifying forces in our system has disappeared.

Moyers suggested in the interview with Burns that the only way to solve serious national problems would be through a collaborative effort on the part of all of government. Burns declined the suggestion:

> The way we get concert in this system is by following a middle way that makes it easier for the different parties and branches of government to cooperate — but the middle way is often not a very effective way. It's not able to deal with something like the deficit,

26

for example. One could mention half a dozen other problems, like the environment and poverty and so on, that the system simply cannot deal with.

What Burns wanted more than anything else was a "strong party system with a President-centered party that would mandate an awesome amount of philosophy and program direction to the country so that the government could act more forcefully over a shorter period of time."

Of course, what Burns and others want is strong political party accountability and government performance. In fact, he went on to say that "when one party gets control of all branches of government, that party is responsible. It's the party you can happily kick out if they don't do the job."

However, it doesn't appear that our country is supporting unified control any longer, and a more realistic appraisal should now be made by its proponents.

New Research, New Times

Mayhew and Fiorina have challenged the president-centered "responsible-party" model of government accountability. They have questioned the prevailing elitist model of government performance in a unified party system, believing that contemporary government has been replaced by a newer "coalition government" model. Voters may have, in a new mind-set, replaced the model of the first and middle parts of the century with a newer model for the twenty-first century.

At this time in our history, the voting public typically is choosing to split control between the political parties of our governing institutions, and we're only now beginning to understand and explain this occurrence. We know that divided government is not new to this nation, but most people do not realize the consistent and pervasive pattern of divided government we've experienced in the latter part of the twentieth century.

Also, it is worth noting that most of the world's democracies are in fact governed by coalitions, which is a form of divided government. The United States system seems to be tracking well with these multiparty Western democracies, even though the American system is highly programmed for only a two-party system.

Party Decline, Split-Ticket Voting, and Divided Government

When we analyze trends in the twentieth century, we identify a strong direction from 1900 through 1952, with twenty-two unified governments and only four divided governments in the United States. However, between 1952 and 1996, there were only seven unified governments, but fourteen divided governments. The latter part of the twentieth century completely reverses the trend from the beginning of the century.

The Political Control of the U.S. Government
(By Session)

The First Half of the Century

Unified Control (22)	Split Control (4)
1901-11	1911-13
1913-19	1919-21
1921-31	1931-33
1933-47	1947-49
1949-53	

The Second Half of the Century

Unified Control (7)	Split Control (14)
1953-55	1955-61
1961-69	1969-77
1977-81	1981-93
1993-95	1995-98

Source: The Roper Center

We know that ticket-splitting as a national phenomenon increased sharply from the mid-1960s through the mid-1980s and has continued to the present day. We also know that a preferred result

28

during this period has been a Republican president and a Democratic-controlled Congress. It appears that that particular trend has been reversed in the 1990s, with a Democratic president and Republican control of the House of Representatives — and the votes in the national electorate seem to underscore this, as the Republicans have increased their congressional vote percentage to a level that has not been seen since the 1920s.

Paralleling the national shared power model for a new "coalition government" have been the results at the state legislative level. It appears to be a universal pattern of decision making that has engulfed not only the national government, but the individual state governments as well. At one time, people tried to isolate the state split control as simply an outcome of the once-solid South becoming more competitive, but that's been rejected by most political scientists.

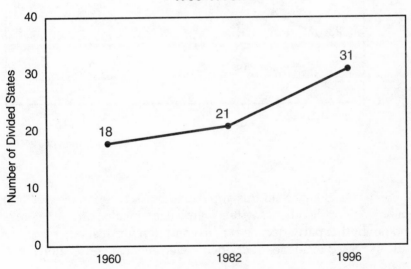

**Divided State Government Control
1960-1996**

Source: The Public Perspective, The Roper Center (Dec/Jan 1997)

Thus, in the last fifty years of the twentieth century, a critical minority of voters have decided to split their tickets between president and their U.S. representative and also between governor and their state legislator, and even to alternate between Democratic and Republican senators from their own state. By 1996, more than thirty states had divided power between the party of the governor and that of the state legislature.

States with Split-Party U.S. Senate Delegations
1950-1996

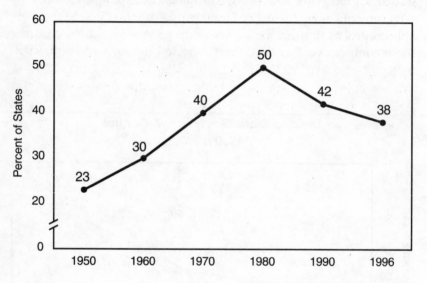

Source: The Statistical Abstract of the U.S.

Some elites have said this appears to be "schizophrenic electoral behavior" while others say it is a very explainable pattern. There is no doubt that party decline is a precondition for this rather systematic increased incidence of divided government at both national and state levels.

"With the realignment theme pretty much played out," Fiorina writes, "divided government has the potential to become the new organizing principle of research in American politics in the 1990s."

Party decline and the rise of divided government was predicted nearly two decades earlier by political scientist James L. Sundquist in *The Future of American Political Parties*.

There remains one final consequence of party deterioration to mention. That is the unprecedented tendency, in the past thirty years, for the electorate to place one party in control of the executive branch and the other in charge of one or both houses of Congress. As party organizations have declined and voter attachments have weakened, voters have come to pick and choose on the basis of the varying appeal of individuals and split their tickets without misgiving — and the ballot reforms and anti-party doctrines that have prevailed since the Progressive era have encouraged them to do so.

Ticket-splitting has been a strong factor in American politics in this last half-century, and we need to now address the power of this pivotal voter in the following chapters.

CHAPTER THREE

The Phenomenon
of Ticket-Splitting
Continues

The 1972 book *The Ticket-Splitter* identified a new model of political behavior supporting a development in the American electorate that is now taken for granted: that certain pivotal voters were
making their choices for individual candidates rather than for the
political parties that had nominated those candidates. The findings
reintroduced to the American campaign the strategic complexities
of independent voting behavior. The ticket-splitter concept has since
been validated and used as an explanatory and predictive tool by
scholars, pollsters, campaign consultants, and news media analysts.

The old models of single-party control of all the branches of
government no longer work for the sake of accountability and
agenda setting, and have not for years; and it is most unlikely that
we will return to straight — behavioral — voting patterns any time
in the future.

The phenomenon of ticket-splitting identified in 1972 has continued, and increased, at all levels of government. Witness the pro-
liferation of shared-control state governments over the last twenty-
five years. Ticket-splitting is even moving into the local levels, which
used to be bastions of one-party strength. Thus, this pattern is running the length of the ballot even in southern states.

Today, voters essentially have balanced their allegiance between the two major parties. In the 1996 national campaigns, the aggregate votes ran approximately 50 percent for Clinton, 50 percent against Clinton, and in the U.S. House elections, 50 percent for Republicans and 50 percent for Democrats. This leaves a key group of ticket-splitters with the deciding voice in competitive elections.

1996 National Election Returns (major party)

	Clinton	**Non-Clinton***
U.S. Presidency	47,400,000	48,900,000
	Democrat	**Republican**
U.S. House	43,600,000	43,900,000
U.S. Senate	24,000,000	24,800,000

*Combined Dole and Perot votes

Congressional Quarterly, 2/15/97

David S. Broder, twenty-five years ago in the foreword to *The Ticket-Splitter*, questioned the merit of ticket-splitting and even the relevance of political parties, echoing the concern expressed in his own book, *The Party's Over* (1971).

"Our concentration on the political parties seems increasingly irrelevant, as the evidence mounts that very little in American politics can be explained in party terms," Broder wrote. "For half the time I worked in Washington, we have had a President of one party and a Congress of the other; what relevance, then, has the idea of party responsibility?"

Since those words were written, not only has the number of voters who say that they split their tickets — and do so — increased greatly, but they have become a third force in American politics — one, in fact, that is deciding most elections in this nation.

An Increasing Perception of Ticket-Splitting

Whether or not they actually split their tickets in the voting booth during the past thirty years, more and more voters, in fact, think of themselves as ticket-splitters.

Since 1968 — a pivotal year in American politics — a trend has developed in which a majority of Americans now say they vote for different parties' candidates for president from one election to another.

Ticket Splitting (Self-Described)
1952-1966

''Have you always voted for the same party or have you voted for different parties for president?''

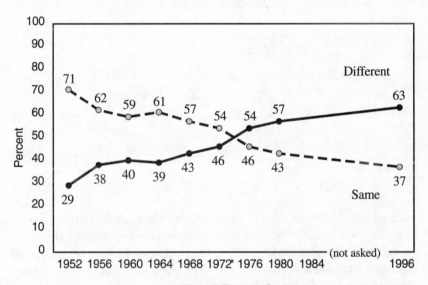

* Pivotal Election Cycle

Source: The University of Michigan: The Roper Center

Ticket Splitting: A History

"Do you usually vote straight ticket, that is, one vote for all the candidates of one party, or do you split ticket, that is, vote for some candidates of one party and some of the other?"

Source: The Gallup Organization (7/16/42)

1942

Straight ticket 58%
Split ticket 42%

"How often would you say you vote a straight party ticket — often, occasionally, or hardly ever?"

Source: ABC/Washington Post (7/28/83)

1983

Often 25%
Occasionally 23%
Hardly ever 52%

"When voting in elections do you typically vote a straight ticket . . . or do you split your ticket?"

Source: The Roper Center (2/96)

1996

Straight ticket 29%
Split ticket 71%

The historical relevance of the 1968 presidential election set a new trend for ticket-splitting that lasted a full generation, and the 1992 election may have signified a new stage of split-ticket voting. These elections signal the increasingly fragmented party system evolving through the latter part of this century.

Writing in January 1997, as the new Congress was convening, Broder systematized the prevailing views of political opinion makers.

But there are more deep-seated problems that are likely to interfere with significant action on the nation's needs in the next few years — problems that are inherent in the political system itself and not peculiar to this president or Congress.

In my view, the most serious of these structural problems is the growing power of interest groups and the declining status of political parties. Parties were born in the first decade of the Republic as a device to mobilize energy and public support sufficient to overcome the checks and balances built into our Constitution. Throughout history, it has been the electoral mandates achieved by strong parties that have produced great policy breakthroughs — whether it was the New Deal, the Great Society or, more fleetingly, the Reagan and Gingrich revolutions.

But parties have lost their legitimacy in the eyes of millions of independent-minded voters, thanks in part to the dominance of television in our suburban-centered campaigns. . . .

The parallels between 1968 and 1992 are significant. Electoral dissatisfaction was demonstrated in 1968 with the introduction of a third-party presidential candidate, George Wallace, who garnered nearly 10 million votes; and this marked the beginning of ticket-splitting as an electoral phenomenon. By 1992, the voting trends of the American people had evolved to a point where another third-party candidate, Ross Perot, was welcomed as a serious contender, garnering nearly 20 million votes. Perot's candidacy detonated traditional patterns of voting, likely impacting those patterns for many years to come.

Historical Perspective

Research conducted over the years shows that straight Democratic and straight Republican voting is decreasing and that ticket-splitting is up. For example, in a 1942 Gallup Organization survey, 58 percent of the Americans surveyed said they "usually vote a straight ticket, that is vote for all the candidates of one party," while 42 percent said they voted a split ticket, "that is vote for some candidates of one party and some of the other." Thus, just one generation earlier, straight-ticket voting was still the norm in American politics.

By 1983, ticket-splitting was becoming entrenched. An ABC News/*Washington Post* poll conducted in the summer of 1983 reported that 52 percent of those surveyed said they "hardly ever" voted a straight ticket, while 23 percent said they did it occasionally and 25 percent said they "often" split their tickets.

Finally, in a 1996 survey by the Media Studies Center of the Roper

Center, the respondents were asked: "When voting in elections do you typically vote a straight ticket, that is for candidates of the same party or do you typically split your ticket — that is, vote for candidates from different parties?"

Voted Split Ticket   71%
Voted Straight Ticket   29

Thus, the trend of ticket-splitting has grown from a level of 42 percent of the electorate a generation ago in 1942 to 71 percent in 1996. Americans clearly perceive themselves as a nation of ticket-splitters, as more than two of three voters claim to split their tickets in the voting booth.

Ticket-Splitting: President–House Elections
1952-1996

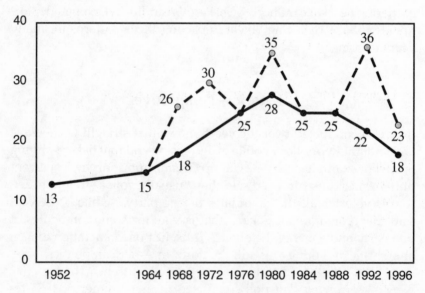

Note: Dotted lines include Third Party splits
(1968, 1980, 1992, 1996)

Source: Morris Fiorina, Harvard University

38

Despite the strong opposition of political party officials, California voters have demanded a "blanket" primary election format which essentially erases any impediment to ticket-splitting. Voters in 1998 became able to vote for any candidate running for a statewide or federal office, regardless of the candidate's political party, eliminating the requirement that Republicans vote only for Republican candidates, and Democrats vote only for Democratic candidates. This development essentially rewrites the traditional campaign rule books and creates concern among politicians worried about losing control of their party nomination process. Ticket-splitting, as a policy formally endorsed even in the primaries, has arrived as a powerful force in California.

But, what about the way the American electorate *identified themselves* with the two political parties from 1968 to 1997? In the years that the Gallup Organization has been measuring Americans' perceptions of whether they are Republicans, Democrats, or Independents, they validated that the greatest shifts have occurred in the 1980s. The Republican party has gained a few points, to about 31 percent; the Democrats have lost a significant ten points, from 43 percent to 33 percent; and the Independents have made a slight gain, from 28 percent to 32 percent.

Political Party Identification (Self-Perceptions): 1968–1998

"In politics today, do you consider yourself a Republican, Democrat or Independent?"

Date	Republican	Democrat	Independent
July, 1968	29%	43%	29%
July, 1972	27	45	28
July, 1977	21	51	28
June, 1989	32	33	30
June, 1993	30	34	33
February, 1997	31	33	32
April, 1998	32	33	35

The Gallup Organization

Writing for *The Ticket-Splitter* in 1972, Broder pinpointed the missing link in political analysis when he emphasized the importance of evaluating actual voting behavior versus voters' stated perceptions of party affiliation:

> The concept of independents used in the University of Michigan studies (and also in Gallup's and Harris's polls) is based on self-perception and self-description. They are the voters who call themselves independents, rather than Democrats or Republicans. On the other hand, the concept of ticket-splitters used in this book is based on voters' behavior, being defined as those who move back and forth across the ballot rather than voting exclusively for candidates of a single party. The two are not identical.

The key finding, as substantiated by the 1996 Gallup post-election survey, is that both parties have now achieved parity in the number of voters who perceive themselves as Democrats (37%) and Republicans (37%), while those who think of themselves as Independents (26%) has remained pretty much the same. Among ticket-splitters, 26 percent perceive themselves as Republicans and 26 percent perceive themselves as Democrats: a total of *52 percent of the ticket-splitters identify with the two major political parties.* The other half of the ticket-splitters (48%) view themselves as Independents.

Profiles of the Ticket-Splitters:
A Thirty-Year Comparison

A key research instrument used for the findings derived for *The Ticket-Splitter* was a 1967 national survey of 1169 voters conducted by Market Opinion Research of Detroit. The changing profile of the ticket-splitter can be portrayed by comparing that research with new research conducted by the Gallup Organization after the 1996 elections.

Ticket-Splitter Demographic Characteristics: 1967–1996

	1967 Ticket-Splitters (N=245)	1996 Ticket-Splitters (N=263)	Significant Change
Age			
18–29	15%	15%	
30–49	42	51	+9
50–64	29	17	
65 years and older	14	17	
Sex			
Female	43%	50%	+7
Male	57	50	
Race			
White	92%	95%	
Black	5	1	
Asian/Other	2	4	
Education			
High School or less	68%	40%	
Some College or more	32	60	+28

In those cases where we could make demographic comparisons, the ticket-splitters of 1996 were more likely to be 30 to 49 years of age, female, and white and to have more formal education (28 percentage points higher) than the ticket-splitters of 1967. Of course, educational attainment has significantly increased among the population at large over the last thirty years, and ticket-splitting reflects that national trend.

The Effect of Ticket-Splitting on the 1996 Elections

An in-depth study of the ticket-splitter vote was undertaken in the 1996 Gallup post-election survey. These were voters who split their ticket, voting for the president from one political party and for a member of the House of Representatives from another. Two important conclusions can be seen from the following table. One was the strong shift between the pre-election intended vote for Congress and the actual vote reported in the post-election survey. Ticket-splitters were dividing their vote nearly equally between the Republican and Democratic House candidates in the pre-election period, but moved heavily toward Republican House candidates by election day (a shift of 17 points to Republican House candidates).

	Total (N=1360)	Ticket-Splitters (N=263)
Pre-Election Vote Intention (Congress)		
Republican House	48%	47%
Democrat House	46	43
Not sure	6	10
1992 Vote Recall		
Bush	36%	27%
Clinton	38	33
Perot I	10	23
Not sure/Did not vote	16	17
1996 Presidential Vote		
Clinton	48%	37%
Dole	43	17
Perot II	9	46
1996 Congressional Vote		
Republican	52%	64%
Democrat	48	36
Time of Decision		
Last days/last week	16%	36%
Earlier than that	83	63
Not sure	1	1

Ticket-Splitters as Skeptics

It is clear in every one of the measures of alienation that the 1996 ticket-splitters voting for president and U.S. Congress have high levels of skepticism about their government. Two-thirds think public officials don't care about them. Eight out of ten think elected officials in Washington are concerned only about their re-election. Nearly three-quarters think government is run by the big interests.

By a significant 10 percent difference, ticket-splitters expressed to Gallup interviewers, in their responses to the following statement, increasing alienation:

``Public officials don't care much what people like me think.''

	Total (N=1360)	Ticket-Splitters (N=263)	Significant Difference
Agree	55%	65%	+10
Disagree	42	34	
Don't know	3	1	

They evidenced an 8 percent difference over the electorate at large when asked to respond to the following:

``Elected officials in Washington care more about getting re-elected than doing what's right for the country.''

Agree	73%	81%	+8
Disagree	25	19	
Don't know	2	—	

Lastly, there was a significant difference of 7 percent concerning special-interest control of government.

``Would you say the government is pretty much run by a few big interests looking out for themselves or that it is run for the benefit of all the people?''

Big interests	63%	70%	+7
Benefit of all	30	25	
Don't know	7	5	

When 20 Percent Takes All

The 1996 elections resulted in nearly 20 percent of the voters splitting their tickets for shared power and thus deciding the outcomes of the presidential and congressional contests. Exclusive data from Gallup and the Tarrance Group present an interesting picture of the electorate leading up to the election day.

	Pre-Election Tracking Polls Tarrance Hotline (N=8,000) Sept. 3–Oct. 31, 1996	Post-Election Poll Gallup (N=1630) Nov. 3–7, 1996	Political Significance
Straight Democrats	44%	41%	-3
Straight Republicans	39	40	+1
Clinton-Republicans	8	7	
Perot-Republicans	4	5	
Dole-Democrats	3	3	
Perot-Democrats	2	4	
Ticket-Splitter Coalitions			
Subtotal	17%	19%	+2
Total	100%	100%	

This Gallup post-election national survey yielded 41 percent who voted for Clinton and a Democratic candidate for the U.S. House and 40 percent who voted for Dole and a Republican candidate for the U.S. House — essentially 80 percent voted a straight-party ticket for president and Congress. The balance of the electorate was approximately 19 percent, splitting their choices between the parties for presidential and U.S. House candidates.

When one considers that the 1996 election total was approximately 96 million voters, the ticket-splitter subgroup in these elections is approximately 17 million voters, and growing. What is even more pivotal to the future is the combined impact of the Clinton-Republican and the Perot-Republican ticket-splitters. Their 12 per-

44

cent of the electorate computes to a healthy 11 million or more voters who can make or break the two major parties in national elections.

In the *Almanac of American Politics — 1998*, Michael Barone drew insightful notice to this new and fragile balance of power.

> So what was the mandate? Clinton and congressional Republican leaders talked after the election about how the voters were demanding bipartisan cooperation. But cooperation for what? It is important here to understand one more thing about the election. The Democratic president's victory looked large, but it was contingent. It depended on decisions that could very easily have gone either way. . . . The Republican Congress's victory looked narrow, but it was fundamental. It was based on a wider than generally appreciated acceptance of its policy thrusts.

A look at the research from the 1996 elections lends some answers. Special in-depth interviews (IDIs), conducted with those respondents to 1996 Gallup post-election polls who voted for divided government, provide even more insights into the mind of the American electorate.

The 1996 voters in this focused research were also asked if they favor a unified, president-centered political party controlling all of government, letting the voters decide in the next election if they want to keep the particular party in power. The intent of the question was to gauge support for single-party control. These voters were virulently opposed to one-party control.

> ``Do you think in the future we ought to have a `unified, President-centered' political party controlling *all* of government and then let the voters decide in the next election if they want to keep that party in power?''

"I think we have the best form of government possible, right now, and we don't need to change it," answered a retired veteran from New Jersey. "I think it's well balanced, it works well."

"No. If one thing goes wrong, and you have a new party, it doesn't mean you fix the problem," responded Elizabeth, a 31-year-old single woman who considers herself "nationalistic" and proud of

45

what differentiates America from other countries. "To make the assumption that the people in power are in control is against my religion!"

"I don't think so," said Kelly, 34, who works in nuclear medicine and considers herself a Democrat. "If the presidential party, whichever party it is, is not in control of the House, there's a lot of publicity. There is a difference of opinion that gets the people who pay no attention whatsoever to politics in on it. Controversy is good when it actually gets them interested."

"I'm not a party man, myself," replied a 34-year-old electronic engineer who said he intentionally voted for divided government when he chose Clinton and a Republican House candidate. "But occasionally I will vote according to party lines if I'm not real familiar with the candidate. I think that having multiple parties is beneficial, just like I think it's beneficial to have two places to go buy hamburger. It provides motivation to provide the best for the most."

"I feel it would be too locked in," replied Lynette, 29, from New York, who says family issues are of primary importance to her. "On certain party issues, it would be too influencing. Too powerful for one party."

"No, I don't think there should be one power there," said a retired North Carolinian who says he's a Democrat but votes "for the man." "That would be just like having a dictator. It's better to have two parties so you have two sides to it and make them compromise on things."

A 34-year-old cabinetmaker from New Jersey was opposed to a clean sweep of the legislature. "You know why? If there's somebody good in there, you want to keep the good that's in there, you don't want to get rid of the good, too. You want to get rid of the bad, or the nonproducing, but you want to keep the one that's producing."

Mike, a 46-year-old unemployed electrical engineer from Texas, said he voted for Ross Perot in part because he felt Perot would not be influenced by special interests. His response to the question reflected that concern as well. "No, because of the special interests. I would think over a period of time with a specific president and House that would be retained for that period of time, that they would become influenced by special interests. I think it would bounce between extremes, instead of having a semi-smooth trail to follow."

"I don't agree," replied a 38-year-old Perot-Republican House ticket-splitter, who says as a businessman, he tends to support Republican policies, but his degree in social welfare lends a Democratic twist to his outlook. "For example, in New York we have D'Amato and Moynihan. I think both do very good for the state of New York. If you just had a unified body that controls things, it would be difficult to say what each state can do. I don't believe we should have one party control everything."

"I just don't think it's a good idea," said a 52-year-old woman from Kansas who works in the aircraft industry. "There can be good candidates in all the different parties, and there might be a real rotten one in a party of four or five that you really like. I can compare this to unions. People run on a certain ticket, and some of those people I wouldn't vote for on a bet. You don't get to choose individuals, you pick the slate."

Ticket-Splitters Are Driving the Movement for Shared Control

On the national level, ticket-splitting is wreaking a fundamental change in American government: an evolution of a political party model from one of single-party control of all the branches of government to one of divided control, or shared power, in which one political party controls the White House and the other controls the Congress.

In late September 1997, the Gallup Organization repeated the question regarding divided government. The preference for divided government among ticket-splitters increased dramatically.

The national trends for divided government are clearly demonstrated. Ticket-splitters' views of divided government lend even more insight into this evolving trend, as they support it by more than a two-to-one ratio, 57 percent to 23 percent.

``Do you think it is better for the country to have a President who comes from the same political party that controls Congress, or do you think it is better to have a President from one political party and Congress controlled by another?''

47

	1996 Voters (N=477)	1996 Ticket-splitters (N=104)	1997 Total population (N=1006)
Same party	33%	23%	31%
Different parties	41	57	45
No difference/ No opinion	26	20	24

Today, the nation essentially has balanced its allegiance between the two major parties, leaving a key group of ticket-splitters with the deciding voice in competitive elections. These polling results dramatically demonstrate a new realization that ticket-splitters are driving the current trend for shared power in Washington, D.C.

Ticket-splitters have moved beyond a desire to simply split their ballots on election day to a vital predisposition to effect shared control of the federal government. When asked about their motivations in the IDIs, they expressed some significant opinions that, when examined collectively, demonstrate an important new evolution in American politics.

''Some people say that when *one* political party controls *all* the branches of government — such as both the White House and the Congress — that this unified control will put an end to so-called 'gridlock' or political-party stalemate in Washington, D.C. Others disagree and say that when there is divided government or shared control of government power that the two political parties then must work harder to come to an agreement and the voters watch more closely the performance of both parties. Which view comes closest to yours — the first or the second? Why do you think?''

"We need two sides, actually," replied Vina, 71, from California. "It's impossible for everyone to think the same way, and someone may come up with something better."

"I think they would come to decisions quicker along party lines, but not necessarily the ones that would be good for the majority of people in America," responded Kelly, 34. "Because I think there is

48

a little bit more special influence that can make them lean one way. If it's not divided, they don't have to answer to as many people."

"I agree with both statements," replied a university administrator who tends to favor the responsible-party model of political scientists. "My perception would be, in the course of history, I'm sure there have been times when our country has been well served by unanimity of the presidency and Congress, and times when it's been well served by division. I think there are valid arguments for both."

John from Arizona also saw advantages and disadvantages to unified control. "I've seen it happen where things have gotten through a lot quicker. Things that would not have gotten through. Decisions that were made that would not have been made had there been a divided government.

"I'm not sure that really is the question you're asking. I think the question you're asking is, is that a good thing? Does it facilitate government? If that's the question you're asking, no, I don't think it does. It all depends on what is getting sent through. I hate to be cynical, but most of the time it's a pork-barrel thing. You give me this, and I'll get you that, and we'll both get rich."

"I don't think so," replied a 51-year-old woman from Illinois who serves in local government but is not sure under which party she is registered. "Even people of the same party disagree. That's why there's such a wide range of voting now. Used to be you were a set Democrat or set Republican. Now you might be a Republican and disagree with what other Republicans think, and vote with the Democrats."

"I agree that the statement is true, that if you have unified control, you will avoid a lot of stalemates in government; however, I disagree with the premises behind it," replied Marshall, a 31-year-old health care worker from Ohio. "I just see it as a more open forum. Divided control makes the two parties work together toward a conclusion and look at the pros and the cons of an issue. As you do that, you may sway the party that was negative toward the issue, you may sway them toward your direction as they see it from a different point of view.

"Also, divided government is going to make the voters more aware of what is going on. If he [a politician] views the issue from a different standpoint than the voters might normally think he would, then he might have to state why he voted as he did. And that can also change the view of voters."

"It's checks-and-balances system like we were talking about," said Rae, 52, to support her position. "Generally speaking, the Republicans are not going to go along with the Democrats. So they have to dig up the support. So there's more time for them to consider whether they've done something right or wrong; there's also more time for them to shilly-shally around. I think basically, it's a good thing."

"You need debate to have democracy," responded a 32-year-old salesman from Houston. "It's not easy to come to a decision, so you need that debate. You need people with differing opinions."

"I think with a Democrat in the White House and a Republican Congress, the public's going to watch more closely," said a 33-year-old woman from Michigan who favors the additional checks and balances divided government brings. "It's almost anti-American to have one party controlling everything."

Delores, a 54-year-old Hispanic who voted for Perot and a Democratic candidate for the House, supported divided government for the media attention it generates and the opportunity for public discourse. "We hear what they say when they're working on the issues," she said. "Then we have the debates between them, which gets into media and then we can pay attention and see, this one wants this, and this one wants that, so what do I want? You have a way of choosing sides."

A cabinetmaker from New Jersey also preferred the additional checks and balances inherent in shared control. "They have to work together to come to an agreement. It seems like they go to extremes. One party is extreme in one direction, while the other goes to the extreme in another direction. When you put them both together and they have to work together, then they work as individuals on their views, and can come to a compromise."

"I think they do work harder together, because they know they're being watched by the people," responded Sally, 65, recently retired in Maryland, who considers herself an independent and voted for Perot. "Like when they were shutting down the government because they couldn't work out a budget. They made such a mess out of it, so they knew they had to work together to come to some agreement. And I think they try harder, and get the pros and cons."

Mike, an unemployed electrical engineer from Texas, supported shared control. "I either don't believe what I'm being told or to me it doesn't make sense. So if one party got control of both the White House and the Congress, if they followed through, it is not what I'd want from government. They essentially tell you what they think you want to hear for them to get elected, and then they do what they want to do afterwards. [With divided government] they still may not do what they say they're going to do. But if they're hashing [the issues] out in a public forum, they're more likely to get to the root of the problem, and at least attempt to solve it then."

"I think the voters do watch more carefully," said Darlene, 66, who is divorced and works for a CPA firm. "Here in Illinois we have the situation with the governor of one party and the legislature being another. It seems like they were in gridlock. But the people just got so fed up that they came down hard on their legislators and they were forced to do something. And the gridlock ended. There are many checks and balances with having that sort of thing."

"That's one of the reasons the Vietnam War was accelerated," said Paul, 38, and a sales representative in the computer industry who voted for Perot. "Because Johnson was in with a Democratic Congress, they kept sending people over and didn't question it.

"Take the Republican Congress the first term of Clinton, where Gingrich got a lot of stuff passed. Yet, we still had some gridlock and the budget wasn't passed, and they began to ask, how are we going to work this out? And they did work it out. So it did give people an interest to see how they do work together.

"I think also the dissatisfaction and the reason for the third party that Perot had gotten involved with has resulted in more independent people in Congress than we've had before. I think people want people to get along and work together. I think we have a lot of new people who do not toe the party line, and basically stood on their own merits. It's not like the machine brought them into power and they owe something to the machine."

The question Broder raised in 1972 is still valid: Is shared power good for the country? Or is ticket-splitting a costly political habit, limiting government's ability to resolve vital issues?

"It is clear that party affiliation is a fragile basis for attempting to explain the mood to predict the behavior of the voters," Broder wrote in *The Ticket-Splitter*. "I think it needs to be considered whether ticket-splitting is a costly political habit — costly in terms of the effect it has on the capacity of government to resolve those issues which aggravate and frustrate our people."

In fact, the federal government in Washington in the late 1990s has finally begun to do just that — resolve those issues that have been aggravating and frustrating the American electorate for nearly three decades. Respondents to our IDIs stated an ongoing dissatisfaction that motivated their vote for shared control; and when presented with the theory that effective resolutions were being reached as a result of shared control in Washington, they expressed an overwhelming endorsement of that effect.

The two coalitions energizing the shared control movement are those who voted for Clinton for president and a Republican for Congress and those who voted for Perot for president and a Republican House candidate. Combined, they make up a significant 12 percent of the electorate and are proving to be powerful agents for change.

CHAPTER FOUR

The Ticket-Splitter Coalitions

Ticket-splitting in the 1990s has become more complex and more differentiated. There is no "typical" national ticket-splitter, just as there is no longer an "average American." Ticket-splitting was high in the 1992 and 1996 elections, at 19 percent of the total electorate, largely because of the third-party movement financed and directed by Ross Perot. This 1996 three-way split at the presidential level increased ticket-splitting as it offered more possible combinations of votes. After the 1996 election, it became clear that four coalitions of ticket-splitters were creating new pressure points on the political system:

- The new status quo ticket-splitters — 7%: those who voted for Clinton for president and a Republican for House
- The new reform ticket-splitters — 5%: those who voted for Perot for president and a Republican for House
- Other ticket-splitters: Dole for president vote and a Democratic House vote — 3%
- Other ticket-splitters: Perot for president vote with a Democratic House vote — 3%

1996 Voters: Partisans vs. Ticket-Splitter Types
(President–House)

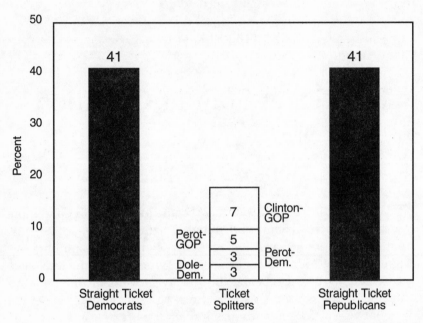

Source: The Gallup Organization (Post-Election Survey)

The first two groups represented 12 percent of the national voters in 1996. The other 6 percent represented less conventional ticket-splitters. The combination of these four ticket-splitting groups adds up to nearly 20 percent of the electorate, a percentage consistent with historical patterns. The ticket-splitters who voted for Clinton for president and a Republican member of the House — those who "got it right" — were the largest and key bloc, at approximately 7 percent of the total vote in the 1996 presidential elections. The Perot and Republican House ticket-splitters made up the second highest percentage, at about 5 percent, and proved to be among the more pivotal voters in this decade. The Dole–Democratic House ticket-splitters and the Perot–Democratic House ticket-splitters each accounted for 3 percent.

The Clinton–Republican House ticket-splitters and the Perot–Republican House ticket-splitters — 12 percent of the electorate — were the most significant agents of change in the election. The Clinton–Republican House ticket-splitters, who took strength from the top of the Republican ticket, have "pushed" the political system. They are forging a new status quo of bipartisan cooperation, while the Perot–Republican House ticket-splitters have added to the Republican base vote and "pulled" the system into reform and change. These two groups of ticket-splitters are twice the size of the other two groups of ticket-splitters, which may be classified as "deviant," in that their choices in the national elections were so much at odds with the outcome.

Approximately 80 percent of America voted a straight-party ticket for president and House of Representatives. This powerful bloc of straight-ticket voters constitutes a large and stubborn base of support for each party's policies. Nevertheless, the two sides are so evenly matched that the ticket-splitters are left to carry the critical balance of power in the election outcome.

On November 9, 1996, the Associated Press issued an analysis of a Voter News Service exit poll of more than 15,000 voters nationwide, in which they were quite straightforward in their analysis of the ticket-splitting decisions in the 1996 presidential elections. "Voters who supported Republicans for the House, but not the White House, made their ticket-splitting decisions later, and favored smaller government. These voters who voted to keep government divided also were more likely to support the incumbent in House districts where one was running." The Associated Press went on to say that these ticket-splitters helped keep Republican control of the House and that the Democrats fell short in their bid for the House majority largely because 15 percent of the Clinton voters backed Republican House candidates. This report explained how Clinton was able to retain the White House in 1996, yet was unable to create a "unified party" for his political agenda in the Congress.

In the in-depth interviews (IDIs) of ticket-splitters that were taken after the election, respondents were asked how they felt about the idea of divided government.

"It may be a slower process to have divided government," one respondent said, "and it may not be as effective, but it is better because of the increased interaction between the two political parties. And the increased scrutiny by the public should make the legislators look at more angles."

Here ticket-splitters, particularly the Clinton–Republican House ticket-splitters, said they liked the idea of divided government because "it allows me to look at the other side's point of view and to open my own eyes."

Another Clinton–Republican House ticket-splitter said, "It's a good idea for divided government because it causes more debate and therefore things are brought out more, and people try to do more. And because of that, the voter can make his own decision, which decision he likes best."

Clinton–Republican House ticket-splitters said that they like to see a "common ground" reached between the two parties, forcing them to come to "agreement and compromise." As another Clinton–Republican House ticket-splitter said, "I agree with what's going on. It goes back to checks and balances. It's important that both parties have to agree on the major decisions and come to a decision on what is best for the country."

The Perot–Republican House ticket-splitters, vital to maintaining the Republican majority in the 1996 House elections, are a different breed. They are "outsiders" in that they follow a pronounced anti-government theme in their verbatim comments. They cast a strong anti-two-party system when they, knowing full well Perot would lose by a large margin, still voted for him. They could well have dropped out of the system, but chose not to do so.

The Perot–Republican House ticket-splitters were even more adamant in their belief that this "new balance of power" in divided government is effective because the parties are forced to come to an agreement on the issues at hand.

One Perot–Republican House ticket-splitter said, "It seems like they go to extremes. One party is extreme in one direction, while the other goes to the extreme in another direction. When you put them both together and they have to work together, then they work as individuals on their views, and can come to a compromise. I know it takes longer to get things done."

Perot–Republican House ticket-splitters also say divided government allows the voters to let the elected leaders know they're "being watched by the people." One respondent said, "Like when they were shutting down the government because they couldn't work out a budget. They made such a mess out of it, so they knew they had to work together to come to some agreement. And I think they try harder, and get the pros and cons."

Another Perot–Republican House ticket-splitter said he liked the idea that the politicians "have to hash things out. They still may not do what they say they're going to do. But at least if they're hashing them out in a public forum, they're more likely to get to the root of the problem, and at least attempt to solve it."

There is definitely a sense of alienation, or skepticism in American government, from the Perot–Republican House ticket-splitters, while the Clinton–Republican House ticket-splitters seem to be a little less strident, and more interested in "increased interaction between the parties trying to achieve a common ground."

Clinton–Republican House ticket-splitters see divided government becoming a sort of gyroscope that maintains a fixed focus or orientation on effective legislation despite inherent party bias. However, the Perot–Republican House ticket-splitters express a skepticism toward one-party control because of their general antiparty attitude. They express more of a visceral feeling about politics, in that they want to "throw all the rascals out" from time to time.

Clinton–Republican House ticket-splitters are "maintaining voters" in that they have voted to continue the current government structure and the control by the two political parties of each of their respective branches of government. In effect, they reaffirmed the 1992 and 1994 election results and thus could be considered "insider voters" insuring the split control of national government.

Convergent Ticket-Splitters, Divergent Profiles

These two key ticket-splitting groups, which more or less maintain the new balance of power in America today, represent divergent demographic profiles. For example, the Clinton–Republican House ticket-splitters are more likely to be female, and by a large margin: approximately 57 percent women to 43 percent men. A surprisingly significant number of women were willing to support Republican candidates for the U.S. House, in spite of the fact that the Republican presidential agenda was not noted for its support of women's issues.

Showing the complexity of independent voting today, the Perot–Republican House ticket-splitter is approximately two-to-one male (65% to 35%), a significant distinction from the more female-oriented Clinton–Republican House ticket-splitters.

Aside from gender distinctions, these two critical ticket-splitting groups are quite similar in other key demographic categories. For example, both Clinton–Republican House and Perot–Republican House ticket-splitters are decidedly white (96% and 94%, respectively) and are younger than the electorate as a whole. About 49 percent of the Clinton–Republican House ticket-splitters were of the baby-boomer generation, between the ages of 30 and 49, which is approximately 4 percent higher than the total electorate itself. Additionally, 53 percent of the Perot–Republican House ticket-splitters fell into the baby-boomer age range, about 8 percent higher than the average in the electorate. Notably, approximately 23 percent of the Perot–Republican House ticket-splitters were among the youngest voters (18–29 years of age), compared to only 14 percent of the country.

The complex makeup of these two types of ticket-splitters has had, and will continue to have, a substantial impact on the direction of electoral politics. Their gender and their youth will strongly influence national elections in the future.

When asked by the Gallup post-election interviewers whether these types of ticket-splitters were conservative, moderate, or liberal, the majority of Clinton–Republican House ticket-splitters chose "moderate" (57% moderate to only 26% conservative). This contrasts dramatically with the largely conservative straight-ticket Republican base vote (71% conservative and only 27% moderate), presenting significant challenges for the Republican leadership to move these particular Clinton–Republican House ticket-splitters into the Republican presidential column in the year 2000.

Approximately 45 percent of the Perot–Republican House ticket-splitters described themselves as more conservative, double the number of Clinton–Republican House ticket-splitters who claimed similar views.

In addition, the Clinton–Republican House and Perot–Republican House ticket-splitters are at great variance in another demographic pattern. When Gallup, in the post-election interviews, asked them whether they identified themselves as Republican, Democrat, or independent, the Clinton–Republican House ticket-splitters leaned toward the Democratic party versus the Republican party by 58 percent to 32 percent, in contrast with the Perot–Republican House ticket-splitters, of whom 70 percent leaned toward the Republican party and only 17 percent toward the Democratic party. These are astounding differences in that both of these ticket-splitters voted for Republican House members in 1996 and both rejected the Republican candidate for president, Bob Dole.

It may be tempting to think these two ticket-splitter types are uninformed and uneducated about politics and government. However, 30 percent of the Clinton–Republican House ticket-splitters had a college or postgraduate degree, as compared to 28 percent of all the voters in 1996. Among Perot–Republican House ticket-splitters, there was a sharp distinction between the men and women, with a surprising 37 percent of the male respondents being college-educated, compared to only 17 percent of the women.

There are differences between the two groups; however, in some ways they are quite similar. For example, the tendency to live in the suburbs characterizes both groups: approximately 48 percent of all Clinton–Republican House ticket-splitters live in the suburbs, as do 52 percent of the Perot–Republican House ticket-splitters. This compares to only 41 percent of the total electorate.

Where the New Ticket-Splitter
Coalition Wants to Take Us

Gallup also asked ticket-splitting voters in 1996 what they thought should be the most important issue for the second-term Clinton administration. They are not single-issue voters; these ticket-splitters mentioned a number of issues and problems. Balancing the budget and education were ranked as the highest concerns. This, of course, represents a good part of the Clinton administration agenda.

Perot–Republican House ticket-splitters were more unidimensional, in that their principal concerns were the budget deficit and balancing the budget. This probably reflects not only an innate preoccupation of these voters, but the Perot campaign rhetoric — paid and unpaid — since 1991. The Perot–Republican House ticket-splitters expressed, at 9 percent, a slightly higher concern for "putting America first," reflecting the isolationist and populist tendencies of this particular vote.

Perot–Republican House ticket-splitters and straight-ticket Republican voters shared support for balancing the budget and reducing taxes, while the Clinton–Republican House ticket-splitters shared the views of the straight-ticket Democrats supporting a balanced budget, health care, and education. This reflects an interesting general divergence of the two ticket-splitter groups between each major party and their long-term goals.

In the post-election in-depth interviews, people were asked whether they felt the complexities of government led them to support shared control.

> ``Do you agree or disagree with the following statement — `I think it is important to try to split the control of the government between the two major parties because the problems today are so difficult to understand and that any mistakes in direction could hurt our country's future'?''

"I disagree," replied Elizabeth, 31, from Connecticut, who considers herself an independent and dedicated voter. "The fact that we trust majority rule means you're not necessarily going to come to the most efficient path. But it's like a pendulum, but sooner or later you'll get there. You may not like who's the president now, but eventually it'll all even out."

"It sounds as if the statement has a certain rigidity to it," responded the university administrator. "Certainly government is complex, although society is complex. I guess I'm not overly impressed that it is so complex and so complicated that it's unmanageable."

"I think our future is really forgiving. I think we could really goof up and it wouldn't be catastrophic," replied John, the electronic engineer from Arizona, expressing an optimistic view of government and the ability of its leadership to cope with its complexities. "I would like to point out that I think bright individuals exist not just in Republicans and Democrats, but in Libertarian and some of the less common parties. People should be seen for the merit of their ideas, not necessarily for the party they belong to."

"I agree. If we're not looking at the broad picture; if we're not looking down the road, we don't have discussions on major issues," said Lynette, a proposal coordinator for an engineering consulting firm. "Again it tends to be very focused, very one-sided. It doesn't allow all of society to offer their opinions or points of view and come to a decision that would be for the good of everyone. I think we need divided control. We need to look at it from both sides. I don't think Democrats or Republicans have all the answers. It's kind of a culmination."

"It goes back to the checks and balances," said Marshall, a 31-year-old sonographer from Ohio. "If you're talking big international decisions, or anything of that nature, it's important that both parties agree or come to the best decision for what is best for the country."

"I really believe that old saying, power corrupts and absolute power corrupts absolutely," responded Rae, 52, from Kansas, who voted for Dole and the Democratic candidate for the House. "So I think any time you have a division of power, it's good. You always have to have two views if you're going to come up with the best answer."

"I think two parties are good," replied Deb, 33, who works as a nurse in Michigan and voted for Perot. "Actually, I think there should be more. There's so much they have to deal with, a multitude of sides that have to be focused on."

"I think it's better with people working together as a team," said Robi, a 44-year-old woman from St. Louis who also voted for Perot. "I think there should be more teamwork."

"The issues are not that hard to understand," responded the 51-year-old wrecker driver from Oklahoma. "All you got to do is set a goal and work toward that goal. The only goal they've set is how much can I put in my pocket this term."

Sally, 65, considers herself an independent and sees positive results coming from a warming relationship between Lott and Clinton. "I think it's important to have the two parties. You get the pros and cons. We have to have the checks and balances so they'll work it out."

"I agree with that," said Vince, married and an involved father of three. "Take welfare reform. I would think we need both parties to work on welfare reform. They have different views and can get together, they can do that check and balance and speak for everybody."

Darlene, 66, agrees that government is complex and can benefit from shared control. "If you make a big mistake, it can affect the whole world, what we do in this country. I think having divided government, even if you have gridlock once in a while, it's a good check and balance."

"I agree," said Paul, 39, and father of three in New York who voted for Perot. "There are no black and white answers. For example, we have a situation with the environment. Vice President Gore is very much pro-environment and he brings a lot to the table. Then you have the Republicans who are very much big business, and saying you can't stifle business. There has to be a happy medium. Then they're forced to work together and find what's best."

The September 1997 Gallup Poll demonstrates the impact the two dominant ticket-splitter groups had in effecting the election outcome that resulted in divided control, with the Perot–Republican House ticket-splitters leading the trend. A significant increase (+12) between Clinton-Republicans and Perot-Republicans shows the volatility of the Perot voter:

"Do you think it is better for the country to have a President who comes from the same political party that controls Congress, or do you think it is better to have a President from one political party and Congress controlled by another?"

	Total	All Ticket-Splitters	Clinton-Republicans	Perot-Republicans
Same party	31%	23%	30%	13%
Different parties	45	57	52	64
No difference/ No opinion	24	20	18	23

The Gallup Organization

Harnessing the Power of the Ticket-Splitter in Campaigns

With 80 percent of Americans voting a straight Republican or straight Democratic ticket for president and the House of Representatives, ticket-splitters become not only important to study but crucial in terms of their significance to election outcomes. Clearly, ticket-splitters in the 1996 election were pivotal to keeping Clinton in the

White House and Republicans in control of the House of Representatives.

Some important differences were found between men and women, even though they come essentially from the same generation. More women supported Clinton for president, with a majority of the Perot supporters being male.

When asked which political party best represents their values, the Clinton–Republican House ticket-splitter showed a fairly evenly distributed response in that 28 percent said Republicans, 35 percent said Democrats, and 26 percent said neither political party did. The Perot–Republican House ticket-splitters, however, overwhelmingly supported the Republican party, by 56 percent, with only 7 percent claiming the Democratic party represented their personal values, while 35 percent said neither.

Thus, these two ticket-splitting groups are going to be hard to combine for the Republican party at the presidential level, but have a greater chance of staying with the Republicans at the House level, as both groups are highly oriented toward a balanced budget and reduction of the federal deficit. That is certainly one of the unifying themes between these two groups.

Moreover, the ability to reach these two voter groups is somewhat different in that 70 percent of the Clinton–Republican House ticket-splitters said they made their voting decisions (for divided government) fairly early in the 1996 campaign, whereas the Perot–Republican House ticket-splitters made their decisions fairly late. For example, almost 50 percent of the Perot–Republican House ticket-splitters claimed they made up their mind to vote for the Republican House candidate in the last week of the 1996 election. This will certainly continue to develop headaches for the Republican House majority leadership in terms of knowing the outcomes of future Congressional elections.

CHAPTER FIVE

The Decade of the Declaration
of Independents

In the early 1980s, Arthur Miller and Martin Wattenberg addressed
the powerful potential of independent voters that continues to
influence elections today:

> Political independence has probably been the most intensely
> scrutinized and debated aspect of the concept of party identifica-
> tion. While the partisan balance has remained relatively stable for
> decades, the proportion of the American population known as
> "Independents" has risen substantially since the mid-1960s. Be-
> cause citizens who do not identify with a political party are gener-
> ally seen as holding the balance of power, such an increase is both
> strategically significant for those concerned with winning elec-
> tions and theoretically significant for scholars concerned with the
> stability of the American party system.
>
> *American Journal of Political Science,* February 1983

The decade of the 1990s differed sharply in terms of independent
voting from the preceding decade, with three noteworthy trends
that have been generally overlooked by observers of American
politics:

- A continued increase in the level of self-classified independent
  voters with a parallel increase in split-ticket voting and the mass

party constituencies at equilibrium, leading to a Congress evenly balanced between the two parties.

- The repudiation in 1994 of the prevailing political system, with the rejection of forty years of Democratic control of the U.S. House of Representatives, replaced by a more populist congressional wing of the Republican party, and its subsequent and significant validation in the succeeding 1996 congressional election.
- The intervention of two Ross Perot third-party efforts, through which millions of voters tried not only to reform the political system, but also to create a totally new movement of participation and action-driven politics.

Rise of the Independent Voter

The identification of public self-perception is an important tool in electoral politics. In 1964, only 22 percent of the electorate, as measured in Gallup polls, said they considered themselves independents, declining to identify with either of the two major party agendas. By 1970, this number had increased to 26 percent of the electorate. Self-described independent voting identification has been on a steady increase ever since. (See chart on page 67.)

In the 1990s, about one-third of the electorate called themselves independents, reaching parity with those who identified themselves as supporters of the two major parties.

Self-Identification Trends

	1964	1970	1989	1997	1998
Independents	22%	26%	30%	32%	35%
Republicans	25	29	32	31	32
Democrats	53	45	33	33	33

The Gallup Organization

Political observers frequently note the significant level of self-perceived independents in our system, but ignore their potential impact as though they were invisible. When a group of voters that do not align with a political system's two major parties reaches such

The Rise of Independents in the Electorate
(Self-Described)

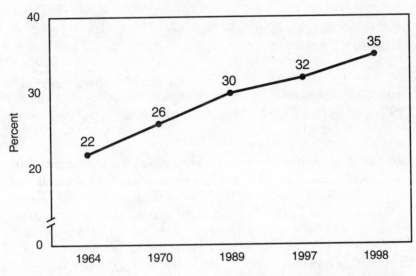

Source: *The Gallup Organization*

a high proportion of the total electorate, the system becomes unstable. Perot's third-party movement underscored this during the decade of the 1990s.

Reversal of Control in the U.S. House

The second important event of the 1990s that differentiated it from the previous decade was the overthrow of the Democratic party majority in the U.S. House of Representatives. This was noteworthy not only because it reversed forty years of control, but because it gave the Republicans control of the purse strings of the government.

Noted political scientist Walter Dean Burnham, in a televised 1997 professional conference, called the 1994 election of a new Republican majority "an earthquake," resulting in a divided government that was "differently put together" than the previous divided government of the 1980s.

U.S. House of Representatives Elections
Majority control = 218

	1970	1980	1990	1996	net change
Republican Members	180	192	174	227	+47
Democratic Members	254	243	259	207	

In the 1980s, while the Democrats maintained their control of government spending as the "congressional party," the Republicans became accustomed to being the "presidential party." The Nixon, Ford, Reagan, and Bush administrations attempted to use this presidential aura to their advantage, trying to bypass the Congress and run the country by the use of television and the power of the veto. An important outcome of such governance was stalemate and gridlock, a consequence of which the electorate clearly disapproved.

In the 1990s, the Republican party was called to take on the responsibility of the congressional party, while the Democrats assumed the role of the presidential party — complete role reversals to the parties' long-time experience and culture. Burnham believes there has been a "new order" created in the political system. This reversal of power in the House of Representatives is but a continuation of that trend.

In addition, secular realignment of voters in the southern states from Democratic party orientation to support for Republicans helped pave the way mathematically toward the new Republican majority in the Congress. Approximately two-thirds of the Republican gains in the U.S. House and U.S. Senate have come from the transformation of party politics in the southern states, which is significant in and of itself.

Perot's Millions

The third, and perhaps greatest, influence on the political development of the 1990s was Ross Perot and his "millions." While the $65

68

million that he personally put behind his third-party effort in 1992 contributed immeasurably to the impact of his movement, the greater influence came from the millions of voters whom he was able to rally around his call for financial responsibility in government.

Perot did more than stir up discontent. In a call that resonated with a record number of voters, he proposed an action-oriented mandate. The American electorate responded, knowing full well the likely outcome and the futility of their choice, but committed to voicing their support for action in Washington. The nearly 20 million votes he garnered in 1992, followed by almost half as many in the 1996 election, set a record for a third-party candidate in the history of this country and unleashed a tremendous force applied in the political arena in the 1990s.

The Third-Party Vote

H. Ross Perot — 1996	8.0 million
H. Ross Perot — 1992	19.7 million
Perot's 1992–96 average	14.0 million
John B. Anderson — 1980	5.7 million
George C. Wallace — 1968	9.9 million

In his 1992 "United We Stand" effort, Perot urged voters to "take back our country," dedicating his program to "the millions of volunteers who accomplished the seemingly impossible task of getting petitions signed. . . . You made it clear that the people, not the special interests, own this country. Everyone in Washington now understands that the American people own this country, have reasserted their roles as owners, and want the country's problems addressed and solved. . . . The founders of our government must be looking down from heaven, smiling on all of you" (*United We Stand*, by Ross Perot).

Scrutiny of the Perot movement presents an important distinction. It was not an antigovernment protest as much as it was antiestablishment, backed by those dissatisfied with the prevailing party elites who had been "getting nothing done." Perot issued a passionate demand for government action, supported by millions of voters who demonstrated true political independence as they opposed the prevailing two-party structure. In effect, the Perot "call to arms" offered voters an opportunity to influence government by voting for increased "checks and balances" on the two major parties.

But Ross Perot's movement called for more than action; it demanded accountability. In his 1992 book, *United We Stand* (subtitled with the challenge: *How We Can Take Back Our Country: A Plan for the 21st Century*), Perot urged Americans to hold candidates accountable by asking them specific questions and requiring specific answers to such problems as the deficit, entitlements, special interests, loss of jobs to foreign countries, and more. He empowered his supporters by convincing them they were the legitimate "owners" of the country and responsible for its performance, much as a business would look to its owners for performance.

Perot outlined in his book five principles:

- "One. The people are the owners of this country. Everyone in government . . . works for the people. . . .
- "Two. All of us must take personal responsibility for our actions and for the actions of our government. . . .
- "Three. We are a single team. . . .
- "Four. We can't keep living beyond our means. The size of government must be permanently reduced. The deficit must be eliminated. . . .
- "Five. Our greatest challenge is economic competition."

This suggestion that candidates should listen to the people rang true for Perot supporters and motivated them to speak up, splitting their tickets for those candidates who they felt would be responsive.

Ross Perot, while generating only 19 percent of the vote in the 1992 presidential election, and half that in 1996, made perhaps a more significant impact on government today than any other single electoral force in the campaigns. His call for action on the national debt and deficit spending motivated an unprecedented number of voters — "Perot's millions" — who changed the focus of American politics in the 1990s, contributing to the following:

- In 1992, the Perot voters helped to elect Bill Clinton president by taking votes from George Bush. They maintained the Democratic majorities in both houses of Congress. And they framed the message for the decade, demanding fiscal responsibility through a balanced budget, deficit reduction, tax reform, reform of welfare, Social Security, and Medicare, and general government reform with a line-item veto and governmental reorganization.

- In 1994, the Perot voters helped to elect a Republican House, or, more precisely, took control from the Democrats, with a campaign that was based on fiscal and reform themes reflected in the Republicans' Contract with America.
- In 1996, Perot voters again denied the White House to the Republican party's "presidential wing." This time, the Perot voters affirmed their support for the new status quo of split control and shared power and protected as well the "congressional wing" of the Republican party in the Senate and the House. The Perot–Republican House ticket-splitter vote was crucial to maintaining control for the GOP in 1996.

While the Perot third-party effort faded, most of its goals were achieved between 1995 and 1997, being absorbed into the two major parties' philosophies as they negotiated shared power in Washington.

The Reform party founded by Perot strives to remain an independent force in the American electorate. Its strategy for the 1998 election, as enunciated in Washington in late 1997, was to "play the role of spoiler in the next year's Congressional elections, which could be the next best thing to winning. The party founded by Ross Perot decided in its national convention this month to target for defeat 50 Republicans in the House of Representatives that it sees as vulnerable, most of them because they were elected by slim margins. The aim is to punish the GOP for blocking reform of campaign fundraising, and for stands on trade and other issues, by knocking off enough Republicans to shift control of Congress to Democrats" (*USA Today*, Nov. 12, 1997).

The *USA Today* story went on to say, "Most political observers believe the Reform Party has so many new hurdles, it cannot possibly maintain its viability. Perot has declined to finance the effort. Third parties generally need a crisis to flourish, and with a strong economy and a nation at peace, there seems to be no such urgency around with which to galvanize support. Reform leaders privately concede one more challenge: It will be difficult to trans-

71

form a party grounded in distrust for politicians and government into a player in the political system."

While the Perot election effort was unsuccessful, it presented another motivation for ticket-splitting. For the first time voters were willing to split their tickets to give voice to their overall dissatisfaction with those running the government. While most Perot voters knew a third-party effort was futile, they chose it as the only recourse available. In fact, this is the interim shift to even more shared-control institutional ticket-splitting.

In the early 1970s, tickets were split to make a pro-candidate statement. Now the pendulum swings opposite as voters split their tickets to issue blanket objections to the choices available: system, parties, platforms. Party decline, ticket-splitting, third parties, and divided government are all manifestations of a new way of looking at modern political power.

> It is an extraordinary act for Americans to vote for a third-party candidate. To do so, voters in the United States must repudiate the current cultural norm and reject or accept the notion that their vote will be "wasted". There is no doubt that this constitutes a "radical act", since loyalty to the two-party system is a central feature of our democracy and has provided the American system with stability not seen in many other countries.
>
> *Third Parties in America, Citizen Response to Major Party Failure,* by Rosenstone, Behr, and Lazarus, 1984

Geopolitically, the Perot phenomenon was evenly distributed across the country. This was not a regional protest. The Perot movement in 1992 received about 4 million votes in the Northeast, about 6 million votes in the Midwest, about 5 million votes in the southern states, and about 5 million votes in the western states.

Perot and the Populist Legacy

Perot delivered into presidential politics an influx of voters who had no strong loyalty to the two major parties but who were attracted by his call to demand responsiveness from elected officials. This trend evidences not only major party weakness that began to develop in the 1980s but also a burgeoning political transformation. It is axiomatic in American politics that there has been a significant up-swing in the mistrust of political leaders, disillusionment with politics, and a feeling of powerlessness on the part of voters. The vast majority of the public have often expressed the view that elected officials in Washington are out of touch with the public and that people like themselves have no say in what government does.

In a November 1996 Gallup post-election poll, respondents were asked to agree or disagree with the following statements:

''Public officials don't care much about what people like me think.''

	1996 Total Voters (N=1973)	1996 Perot Voters (N=129)	Political difference
Completely Agree	15	29	+ 14
Mostly Agree	41	45	
Mostly Disagree	35	22	
Completely Disagree	7	3	

''Elected officials in Washington care more about getting re-elected than doing what's right for the country.''

	1996 Total Voters	1996 Perot Voters	Political difference
Completely Agree	27	46	+19
Mostly Agree	47	42	
Mostly Disagree	20	9	
Completely Disagree	4	2	

The Gallup Organization

The in-depth interviews asked ticket-splitters whether they had confidence in the ability of the two major parties to have full power to govern, or if alienation and distrust expressed itself in a support for divided government. While many did express distrust, it was learned that others split tickets not necessarily from a lack of trust, but from a concern for a balance of policy and support for individual candidates.

``Do you agree or disagree that if there is `divided government'
— that is, when one political party is elected to the White House
as President and another party is elected to the majority in the
U.S. Congress — it signifies a lack of trust in either political party
to have full power to govern?''

"That's certainly not what my vote meant, so I guess I would say, no," said the university administrator. "I was voting more for the person, and the choice I made, while I was not wildly enthusiastic in every case, was the best choice of the two or three names that were on the ballot at any given time. I certainly am frustrated at the seeming inability of folks to work together, and to put partisan politics behind them once they're in office, but we'll have to find a different way to resolve that current shortcoming of our current elected officials."

"I don't really care which party is in power in either case," said a 35-year-old engineer who is a registered Republican. "I prefer that we have a divided government. I don't think it necessarily shows a distrust."

"Not necessarily a lack of trust," replied Deb, the 34-year-old nurse from Michigan, a Perot voter who is studying Native American culture in college. "It's almost un-American to even consider it. Maybe people are just too fearful of giving one party too much power."

"I guess I really don't think so," said a 25-year-old advertising copywriter from Minneapolis. "I vote more for the person than I do the party. I would guess most people among my generation vote whether or not we like the question. I would say no. As far as how I vote, I don't do it out of lack of trust; I just vote for the person rather than the party."

"No. I think basically people look at who's running, and listen to what they say," responded a New York salesman and father of three who voted for Perot. "That's why you have so many split decisions. Nobody's going to accept the party line as much."

Other voters did express an opinion that support for divided government signifies a lack of trust in the political parties.

"Sometimes but not necessarily," replied a 31-year-old woman who describes herself as an independent. "In my town election, I vote Democrat. In my state election, I vote Republican. In the presidency this time, I voted for the Democrat. I trust who I voted for. I don't trust either party, but I may have a little more faith in certain people in a party. I think when they get together in Washington, you can't trust them."

"Somewhat, yes," said a 35-year-old man from Ohio who considers himself a Republican. "If you had an all-Democratic government, then it might be too easy. Things would go through without a lot of checks and balances. I can see where that would be a problem. Especially now I see the government working differently than what it might have been a few presidencies ago. A lot more things seem to be going through Congress than it used to. If you have an all-Democratic or all-Republican government, I can see a lot of things swimming through that should not."

"I think it does," replied a 32-year-old mother of three who works as a manager for a South Carolina printing company. "You don't want the fox guarding the hen house. I think with all the lobbyists and stuff that we have now we would have a tendency to go toward more special interest groups, because a lot of those are party-based. I just don't think that's quite right."

"I guess people don't trust government to have all the authority," responded a 33-year-old man from Texas who voted for Dole. "They want freedom in the United States. They want power in the private sector, not the public sector. They believe concentration of power is corrupt."

"Nobody trusts the government anymore," said Jack from Oklahoma. "It used to be the government of the people, by the people, and for the people. Now it's a government of the politicians, by the politicians, and for the politicians. We have got some politicians that literally run our country. The days of the patriot we had a hundred years ago are gone. I don't believe there's a person up there that's there to help the people."

Presaging the Perot phenomenon in the late 1980s, the Times Mirror company created a new political typology for our political electorate in which they segmented various core Republican groups and core Democratic groups to more accurately reflect the new information age, with an implicit rejection of some of the old demographic labels from the industrial age. One of the more intriguing groups empirically identified was what Times Mirror called the

"Disaffecteds," representing approximately 12 percent of the adult population. They described this group: "alienated, pessimistic and financially pressured, leans toward the GOP camp, but has had historical ties with the Democratic party, and . . . Disaffecteds are skeptical of both big government and big business, but are certainly pro-military."

Trends in Typology Groups

	May 1987	May 1988	May 1990
Disaffecteds	9%	11%	12%

The Times-Mirror Center for the People
and the Press, October 11, 1990

This group was one of eleven political subgroups identified by the survey, and the group that demonstrated the most significant increase over the time measured. The Times Mirror company has not conducted any further typologies since 1990.

Typical Disaffected voters resembled Reagan Democrats who could not maintain a home under the George Bush "establishment" administration and vented their antiestablishment concerns within the Perot movement.

A fitting precursor to this decade of independent thinking was an unpublished and confidential Reagan-Bush Re-election Committee memorandum by Lee Atwater and Jim Pinkerton, issued prior to the 1984 elections and titled "What is Populism?" This monograph suggested that populism represents "a family of related ideas, emphasizing agrarianism, antielitism or both. Populism puts great emphasis on idealizing the common folk and setting them in opposition to the classes above and below them. Populism depends on the mobilization of commoners into a political movement."

Populism, as an expression of independent thinking, purports to represent the interest of the rank and file citizen who is beset by huge and hostile institutions, the authors wrote; and populists believe in "standing up for the little guy," making sure that the little guy "gets a fair shake," and "cutting the big boys down to size."

Other key points from the 1984 campaign memorandum that helped the Reagan strategists maintain support of the Reagan Democrats and other populists included:

- Populists are alienated, angry, resentful, and suspicious. They don't trust large institutions or their leaders. However, populists are intensely patriotic and loyal to an idealized and abstract concept of America.
- Populists are swayed by quasi-mystical appeals to nationalistic and patriotic sacrifice. Concepts like loyalty, will, force, and leadership are extremely meaningful to them.
- Populists are hostile to welfare for the poor, such as food stamps and AFDC. They also oppose "welfare" for the rich, such as IMF loans and tax shelters. However, populists enthusiastically support middle-class subsidy programs, such as agricultural price supports and Social Security.
- To the elite, populists may seem like a fairly unappealing bunch, which is no doubt why they have been so neglected. The last politician to openly and effectively court them was George Wallace. . . . Populists are not organized, but they are too numerous to be ignored.
- Populists are both right and left. They are pragmatists. They want results. Populists are frustrated and impatient. They will not give a new policy or program much time to work. This means that they are never satisfied, that they are usually in the position of opposing the people in power, whatever their ideology. It is typical of populists that their rhetoric and thinking become overblown, overheated, and radical.
- It is important to note that much of the "conservative" strength in the GOP and the nation comes from people and areas that aren't conservative at all, but are radical. The South and West, where leaders such as Ronald Reagan have their base, have been in opposition to the entrenched Eastern establishment since the time of Andrew Jackson. There is a great deal of power in this antiestablishment, antielitist sentiment in the South and West, as the 1980 elections attest.
- At its best, populism stands for self-reliance, decentralization, and open and responsive government. At its worst, populism is chauvinistic, xenophobic, and paranoid.

This campaign memorandum explained why Reagan always had more appeal among populist voters than his party.

> Ronald Reagan has always expressed the best aspect of populism, which is optimism about people. He has always scorned the elitist view of mankind, which is pessimism about people.
>
> The President's outspoken opposition to the "business-as-usual Washington buddy system" and his scorn for "the puzzle palaces on the Potomac" endeared him to the populists.

The memorandum concluded by summarizing the successful strategy Reagan utilized in maintaining his populist support:

> We must emphasize the values that President Reagan shares in common with the American people. Even if the populists have a different policy agenda, they will respect a leader who comes across as one of them at heart.

The populists of the 1980s who supported Reagan found their voice in the 1990s as Perot voters. That voice, and the "United We Stand" movement orchestrated by Perot, was heard by Newt Gingrich and the Republican party as they devised the Contract with America that helped them win a majority in the 1994 congressional elections. And as we approach the year 2000, the struggle continues for the populist soul as a key to the new "independent voters" and their impact on the balance of power in America.

CHAPTER SIX

Shared Power Is Effective but Limited Government

In his December 1997 commentary entitled "Balance of Power" in *Campaigns and Elections*, Ron Faucheux acknowledges the "new equilibrium" in shared control that voters continued to affirm in the November 1997 off-year elections scattered around the country:

> After an election where thousand of candidates, consultants and volunteers beat their brains out to win races that at the time seemed like epic struggles, it's always irksome for these bloodied and exhausted combatants to hear from pundits and analysts that the bottom line of their Herculean effort was . . . the status quo.
>
> But the campaigners of 1997 can take heart. What happened this year may not have brought upheaval to American politics, but it did do something that was both important and interesting: It protected a fragile balance of power between the two parties that has been in existence for the past three years.

Historically, the end of the century signifies a generational change, as though voters are not certain if they want young visionary leadership balanced by gender and race or older experienced leadership. A similar alignment occurred at the end of the nineteenth century, as the economy was shifting from an agricultural age to heavy industry. Now we are seeing a transition from that industrial base to a new information era, or "Internet Age."

In this transitional era of downsizing, deregulation, and decentralization, voters are exploring ways to effect change electorally. They are playing out their insecurities and ambiguities in their electoral behavior by splitting their tickets. And while only 2 percent of these ticket-splitters say they intentionally voted for divided government, a majority, when asked to consider what shared power is bringing in Washington, say they support the results: a government equally balanced between the two major parties, with its actions checked perhaps beyond the parameters set in the U.S. Constitution.

Influence of the Postindustrial Era

In an article written for *The New Democrat* in December 1997, Everett Carll Ladd of the Roper Center for Public Opinion Research examines the contrasts between the end of the 1800s and the end of this century. He explores the emergence of the New Deal era from the maturation of the industrial era, producing an America of "great institutional scale and interdependence . . . marked by the prominent place accorded big-city interests and party organizations, and by the cementing of ties between the party and a growing labor movement." Ladd continues:

> But if the dominant impulses of industrialization were centralizing and government-enhancing, those of the present post-industrial setting are the polar opposite. In the economic and technological spheres, dispersion and decentralization have proceeded apace — making the centering of political power in national government bureaucracies seem increasingly anomalous. . . . We are seeing overall quite an extraordinary movement away from monopolies. Telephone companies are an obvious case in point. . . . Job growth, which has been so impressive over the past 20 years, and continues now in the second Clinton administration, has occurred primarily through a vast expansion of small enterprises. In the face of such social and economic changes, a major political shift was inevitable. The latter has proceeded in stages — centering on a transformation in thinking about what individuals need to prosper — which involves, of course, issues of government's role.

Shared Power Is Effective but Limited Government

The mind-set of the American voters is being redefined as we approach the year 2000. For the last half of this century we have watched voters grow alienated and cynical, resulting in an increase in ticket-splitting and nonvoting. That alienation is evolving, not out of disgust for the process, but out of a demand for more accountability, for more problem-solving action and a new system of "policy balancing."

Skepticism about government continues to grow. Since 1984, Americans have been evenly divided when asked if they favor "smaller government with few services, or larger government with many services." But in the 1990s, the support shifted decisively, by more than two to one, to favoring "smaller government with fewer services."

Voters Want Smaller Government
1988-1996

"Would you say you favor smaller government with fewer services or would you favor larger government with many services?"

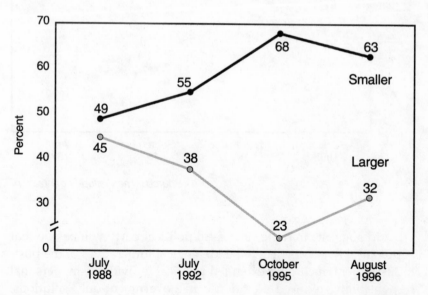

Source: *The Roper Center*

Ladd describes how the social-structural imperatives of the post-industrial era are shaping practical politics, claiming that the contemporary political era rests on a foundation as firm as that on which the New Deal was built, negating many pundits' views that this current support of limited government derived from shared power is nothing more than a "shot-gun marriage" of limited duration.

Voters Want Less Government Involvement

"Some people think the government is trying to do too many things that should be left to individuals and businesses. Others think that government should do more to solve our country's problems. Which comes closer to your own view?"

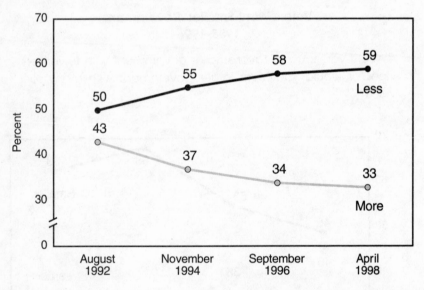

Source: *The Gallup Organization*

Ladd suggests that the successful political party will be one that is prepared to acknowledge the ideological imperatives of the post-industrial era, including extended political individualism, personal responsibility, reduced confidence in government-only solutions, and coalition government.

82

The contemporary era is noted for this resurgence in political individualism, a value on which the country was founded. Voters are less inclined now in the postindustrial era to believe that centralization and greater "program efficiency" are virtues. They feel that for the individual to be strong, government must be limited. In supporting this traditional value, voters are discovering that limited government, as the product of the shared control mandated by the fragile balance of power in Washington today, gives them effective government rather than the gridlock-driven stalemate of the previous decades.

The movement into a postindustrial age and the resurgence of personal individualism continue to influence voters as the traditional concerns of Cold War communism and the budget, deficits, and taxes are being "solved." They are centering their votes more and more around a new set of issues. "Hard" issues include crime and personal safety, responsibility for environmental protection, and difficult economic concerns like the Consumer Price Index, Social Security, and Medicare. "Soft" issues include the family issues focused on education, day care, elder care, and health care.

Michael Barone, in *The Almanac of American Politics — 1998*, says voters are now looking for "order" from government, rather than a smooth business cycle and a redistribution of wealth by the government. He, too, rests his argument on the changing American character as we enter the postindustrial era, likening it to the early 1800s analyzed by Alexis de Tocqueville, before the industrial era.

> The fallacy that the first things most voters seek from government are economic is an idea that grew out of New Deal politics and Keynesian economics — specific responses to an episode of severe economic disorder. . . .
>
> In this new-old America the political rules are different from those most have grown up with and are accustomed to. Underlying much traditional political analysis is the assumption that the first things voters seek from government are economic. . . . But that is clearly wrong. The first thing voters seek from government is order — a rational, predictable order in which ordinary people can raise their families, make their livings, participate in their communities and go about their daily lives without fear of physical disorder or economic disaster.

Arguments about what sound like economic issues are often arguments over cultural issues. Consider welfare. . . . The argument is better portrayed as a battle between one side whose cry is "personal responsibility" and another whose belief is "it's society's fault."

So we are moving from what has been an exception in American political life back to what has been the rule. . . . This is a country in which order exists because basic rules are accepted by the people: from a government in which political forces and governmental mechanisms tend to ratchet down the size of government, not ratchet it up as did the political forces and governmental mechanisms operating from the New Deal years up through the 1980s.

This argument now turns to how some voters intend to check and balance this set of rules in our political system.

Twenty years ago, Martin Diamond's lecture on "The Separation of Powers and the Mixed Regime" to the Woodrow Wilson Center (published posthumously in a 1978 issue of *Publius: The Journal of Federalism*) asserted that many elitist scholars have had an inaccurate understanding of the Founders' intentions in the separation of powers. Diamond argued that unified party control defeats the intent of separation of governmental powers written into the Constitution:

If there is any powerful, distinct, permanent interest in society, adverse to the rights and interests of all the others, and if such an interest were to gain control of all the branches of government, then the separation of powers would be rendered utterly useless. . . . For example, if a single ideological and disciplined political party came to prevail what good would the separation of powers be? . . . Thus we say with certainty that the separation of powers requires that we avoid the emergence and triumph of such a party system. This helps to explain why a preference for such parties always goes hand in hand with a hostility to the separation of powers.

Ticket-splitters from the in-depth interviews reacted to this intellectual argument by Diamond in a way he would not have foreseen.

It was found in the in-depth interviews that a portion replied in constitutional terms, while a majority replied in political party terms.

''When someone from another country describes the United States system of government, they usually point out that the U.S. Constitution has two special features to it: (a) 'The Separation of Powers' and (b) 'Checks and Balances.' What does the first feature mean to you today and what does the second mean to you today?''

"The separation of powers means the people who make the laws aren't the people who administer the laws," replied a 34-year-old man who considers himself interested in national politics and intentionally voted for Clinton and a Republican House candidate because he favored divided government. "And the people who administer the laws aren't the people who mete out justice. Checks and balances are the product of having the division of power provide checks and balances so that one portion or group of people aren't enabled to become too powerful."

"Separation of powers means they watchdog each other," said Kelly, a 34-year-old healthcare worker. "One's responsible for making the laws but not enforcing them. We have checks and balances because there has to be a division of power."

"Checks and balances have to do with the balance of power," according to a 33-year-old nursing assistant from Michigan who voted for Perot. "It's almost necessary to have that kind of separation. Our country was founded on the basis that no one person or individual would have total power. Not even the president of the United States should be above the law."

"By that I think you mean the judicial, legislative, and executive," responded an 87-year-old woman from Arizona about the meaning of the term separation of powers. Checks and balances limit power, she went on to say. "We don't want any one of the powers to become so powerful that the other two wouldn't stand a chance of influencing legislation."

Much like these ticket-splitters, Diamond concluded that the idea of a "mixed regime" was envisioned by the founding fathers in developing the U.S. Constitution. Today, Diamond's concept could be rephrased as "shared power" — within the government and between the major political parties.

What then was this idea of the mixed regime as it was so vividly available to the Americans of 1787? The clue lies in the word *mixed*. It was a regime in which rule did not belong to any single element in the community, but rather was shared or mixed between several elements. . . . The fundamental presupposition was that society was naturally a compound of such radically disparate elements that the political order had to reflect their fundamental diversity. Thus, each fundamental stratum had to have a share in ruling the political community, so as to protect each other from the oppression of the other and to bring into the political community the partial idea of justice which each possessed.

In one of the most important discoveries of this study, it was found many respondents to the in-depth interviews (IDIs) did not have a clear idea of the original intent of the two vital features of the Constitution. They seemed to see divided government as a means to increase separation of powers and assure adequate checks and balances *between the political parties*.

"We cannot give one party all the power. It's better to split it up so one party can check up on the other one," said a 56-year-old Hispanic grandmother from El Paso, Texas.

"If you have split control, they would be more apt to bring out the pros and cons than if you have unilateral control; an increase of checks and balances," according to a 32-year-old Ohio father of one son who feels shared control is resulting in better legislation.

"To me, it's where you have a system where you can keep a person or a party in line," said an Oklahoma City wrecker driver who voted for Perot. "Not to let them get too powerful. When a party or a person gets too powerful, they tend to lose it. They show it. And they use power in a corrupt way. It's just nature. Without checks and balances, the rich are going to get richer, and there's not anything anyone can do about it."

"People from one party being in Congress and the president being of another," responded Darlene, 66, about checks and balances. "Even though it seems like they don't get a lot done, with one party in power, they could just steamroll right on through everything they wanted to do."

Separation of powers limits power, in the view of David, 36, who works in the timber industry of Northern California. "So a dictator or one party doesn't have all the power. And we have checks and balances so no one political view would be constant."

According to Barone, the close election results of 1996 led to this new spirit of competitive cooperation in 1997.

> In the ordinary course of things, incumbents who are reelected to office emerge from the election more powerful and confident than when they went in. But not in early 1997. The 49% president was distracted by scandal. The 49% House Republicans were distracted by something akin to a loss of nerve, a sense that they had somehow lost the election that they had actually won. . . . Leaders of both parties interpreted the election results as a demand for bipartisan cooperation. . . . The voters clearly were in a mood for tranquillity and were tired of what they regarded as bickering.

And the public was in the mood for some action from Congress. Contrary to earlier protest movements like, for example, the George Wallace 1968 American Independent Party, which wanted "government inaction," Perot voters wanted immediate action and control over the establishment.

The IDIs reflect this desire for government action, even if the action taken runs contrary to their personal views. This runs counter to a common assumption that voters who want to limit government would prefer no government action.

``Do you agree or disagree with the following statement — 'I would prefer a government that sometimes acts against my views or wishes than a government that does not act at all'?''

"Yes, I guess I really would," responded Jack, 50, from Oklahoma. "We have had a government that didn't act at all. Eisenhower was a president that didn't really make any bad decisions because he didn't really make any. Carter was another. He made very few decisions. At least a government that makes decisions is trying."

"If they don't act at all, what kind of a government would it be?" said a 72-year-old retired widow from California.

And an 86-year-old grandmother from Arizona: "A government that doesn't act at all would be horrible."

"I can respect a person who tells me they're going to run on a certain platform, and, even though I didn't vote for them, continue to fulfill that platform when elected," replied the Indiana university administrator. "I guess I have enough confidence in the democratic process that I think that's the way the system is supposed to work. Four years later, or two years later, I'll 'seek my revenge' and see if I can influence the direction the other way. Generally speaking, I think it's better to act than not, and have some policy moved forward."

"Absolutely," replied the 34-year-old divorced father of two who works as an electronic engineer. "Why? Well, first off, I could be wrong! If I'm not, there's going to be enough people with my opinion that doing something wrong may galvanize them to become vocal."

"If they didn't act at all, nothing would get done," said a 75-year-old man from North Carolina.

"My view may be negative as a whole to the country," said Marshall, 32, from Ohio. "For example, just because I want an across-the-board income tax at 12 percent, that may be very good for me. But for someone who may be more at the poverty level, that may not be very good for them. Just because it's good for me, it may not be good for the rest of the country."

"The government has to act for everyone, not just for me personally," replied Deb, 33, from Michigan. "What's good for the country isn't always going to be good for me."

"I would have to say I agree with that," said the 39-year-old cabinetmaker from New Jersey. "I'd rather have them do something than nothing. Stagnant water is no good. But, of course, I want them to do what I want them to do!"

"I'd rather, for the foreseeable future, have government run like a business, where the best approaches are determined and followed, and reviewed periodically," responded an unemployed electrical engineer and father of two. "So we are making decisions to get problems solved, rather than just being mired in rhetoric and not taking action to solve anything."

Hallmarks of shared control as it leads to limited government, revealed in the IDIs, include the following:

- more accountability to the voters
- more information to the voters through debate and disagreement
- more competition for new ideas
- more potential for reform
- less stress for the voters in terms of decision making, but
- more stress for leaders who must learn to compromise party and caucus positions

The twenty-first century will become the era of forced compromise, because the parties are so evenly matched. "Checks and balances" will continue to be reinforced to include the two political parties, taking the concept beyond the traditional constitutional structural implications. This newly emerging model of coalition government is providing win/win decision making, whereas traditional political party models of government forced win/lose situations. In effect, America is entering a new era of coalition government similar to the European experiences — except the American experience places a greater value on a more limited government.

This era of competitive cooperation at the national level follows a trend of shared control that has been occurring in state and local governments for years. Currently more than thirty states have elected a governor of one party and at least one body of the legislature of the other party. A new Jeffersonian model of modern American politics is evolving as the federal government transfers money and power to the lower levels, thereby forcing the national government to decentralize and share power once again. This redistribution at the national level of power and resources rather than personal wealth is intentional, and the result is a shifting of the federal government to a lesser role, back to its original role of "referee," rather than following a policy of enlightened elitism.

In fact, in the twenty-first century, the theme of redistribution of political power will replace the theme of redistribution of private property and wealth of the twentieth century.

Why is divided government in the 1990s different from divided government in the 1980s? Because with the end of the Cold War, Republicans no longer find the electorate looking to them to lead the international agenda. Democrats no longer find their position advocating a welfare state salient as we move from a large corporate industrial age into the individualized information age. This transformation of party roles leads the shift to a new era, sparked by Perot's 1992 candidacy, moving the political agenda to one of fiscal responsibility and limited, more effective, government. Democrats and Republicans are finding themselves fighting for a spot in the new national discussions. Failure by either major political party to participate in the discussion could lead to ongoing minority status.

Finally, what does all this say about the elections in the year 2000 and beyond? No longer should parties assume they can achieve ballotwide victory. As a matter of fact, the key voting group — the ticket-splitters — don't want it. For example, should Republicans choose to regain White House control, they may have to be willing to sacrifice control of the Congress. Or they will have to nominate an "outsider" candidate for president, presenting an appeal more similar to Ronald Reagan's candidacy than Bob Dole's. Similarly, for the Democrats to hold on to the White House, they will have to continue to offset the U.S. Congress with a centrist Democrat with "reformist" views.

The 1996 elections were predictable, according to tracking polls. They served to reinstate the new status quo, with Republicans maintaining control of the Congress, despite predictions of an impending shift back to the Democratic party. This can be attributed to three factors: the influence of the Perot candidacy, ticket-splitting, and the coalition government being formed since the passage of welfare reform in the summer of 1996. The November 1997 elections demonstrated the firmness of these trends, and it is expected that the November 1998 elections will do the same, barring any dramatic economic reversals or political resonations in the White House.

Increased checks and balances of the political parties will be a strong force for the foreseeable future. Ongoing research by the Gallup Organization continues to demonstrate public support for divided government, or shared control. Note that unified control was the norm until 1994, with the trend broken then with the overthrow of the Democrats from majority control of the U.S. House of Representatives. The new trend for shared control continues to increase today.

"Do you think it is better for the country to have a President who comes from the same political party that controls Congress, or do you think it is better to have a President from one political party and Congress controlled by another?"

	September 1992	September 1997	April 1998
Same party	47%	31%	40%
Different parties	31	45	42
No difference/ No opinion	22	24	18

The Gallup Organization

At the conclusion of the IDIs, respondents were asked to summarize their impressions about divided government, having spent more than an hour discussing the various aspects relating to it.

"Before our interview today, you likely had not given much thought to the idea of divided government or shared control. Now that you've had some time to explore your thoughts, what is your overall impression?"

"The more I think about it the more I believe in it," said Tina, 31, who voted for Dole and her Democratic candidate for the House. "The best benefit of it is to get people with the different views in there bringing new and different ideas."

"I think it's a good idea," concluded a 34-year-old Clinton-Republican House ticket-splitter. "It's not very cost effective, because everything takes longer; the wheel is slower moving. If patience is a virtue, you're going to have better results coming out."

"It's a good thing," responded Robi, 44, from St. Louis. "It's not going to be a tunnel-vision type of thing. You're going to have different opinions this way. I think it's going in a good direction; it's getting better."

"I was intrigued by your concept that it is a calculated move on the part of the American electorate to provide checks and balances, not recognizing the Constitution already has them in place," said

91

the college administrator from Indiana. "I would not necessarily have given the American electorate that much of a vote of confidence. Generally speaking, all things being equal, I think it would be better if there were some unanimity in the White House and the Congress, but I'm not displeased with the thought that different views and checks and balances that are created even beyond the constitutional checks and balances might be in place."

"We do need it. We need the checks and balances," replied a 65-year-old retired secretary who voted for Perot. "I think I've been seeing it, with Senator Trent Lott. He's been coming around and Clinton's been coming around to him. There have been so many subjects, the budget, the CPI, etc. I don't know if it is all sincere, but I do think it's important to have the two parties."

Shared control or divided government is proving to be effective in governing the country, and it's an idea the voters like. And the more they think about it, the more they like it. It is a result of ticket-splitting, producing an effective, if not fragile, balance of power. This balance has led to a new era of competitive cooperation, forcing the government to produce results and focus on the role of both parties to share the fiscal arena. We envision the future to hold more of the same, barring an economic catastrophe or some such unpredictable event. We see a solid establishment of this new balance of power, maintained by ticket-splitters. This phenomenon will undoubtedly continue to gain support throughout the electorate as more and more voters come to see the inherent benefits that divided government, or shared power, brings to creating an effective, but limited government.

APPENDIX 1

Ticket-Splitting in North Carolina Leads to Divided Government: A Case History

JOHN N. DAVIS

Executive Director, NCFREE
North Carolina Forum for Research & Economic Education, Inc.

Throughout the decade of the 1990s, a scorned mob of ticket-splitting North Carolina voters has been on an antiestablishment tear, ending the century-long domination of the state purse by white, male, rural, conservative Democrats and beginning a new era of diverse leaders in preparation for the next great millennium.

Lifelong Tarheel partisans, broiling with cynicism and confounded by political doublespeak, abandoned traditional party loyalties at the secret ballot box in the first half of the decade and voted to check the unchecked establishment by dividing the state's budgetary power into not just two but three ways. In addition to electing the General Assembly's first Republican-controlled chamber in the twentieth century, voters gave North Carolina's governor veto power, a first in the state's history and the last state in the United States to do so.

Joining this newly emboldened bloc of independent ticket-splitters were over a million newcomers to North Carolina's voter registration rosters, yielding a deadly one-two political knockout punch in the 1992, 1994, and 1996 state political bouts. So intimidating was this new coalition of unconventional voters that the fear of their ire sent North Carolina lawmakers scurrying to enact legislation in all areas of neglected public concern. The number of public policy matters dispensed with during the 1995, 1996, and 1997 sessions of the state legislature was so great that an entire era of previously intractable issues ended successfully.

Now, drawn by the magnetism of a new millennium and the hope it brings for a new beginning, North Carolinians are working to establish a refreshed sense of common identity and purpose and a slate of diverse leaders responsive to a dramatically changing citizenry.

A One-Paragraph History of North Carolina Politics from 1587 to 1990

Once there was a land where right was right and sin was sin and the women, the Republicans, and the people of color were in their proper lower-caste places. It was a land made rich by the sweat of the brow of its salt of the earth people and the providential care of the Good God Almighty who smiled favorably on the tobacco crops and the textile shops year after year until a great wealth was laid up in the storehouses of the blessed. It was they, the blessed, who ruled the day every day. It was they, the blessed, who but for the Grace of God were born white, male, rural, and conservative Southern Democrat. It was they, the blessed, who enjoyed the peace that only comes from being certain that you are among the select few divinely destined for eternal life in heaven and paternal dominance on earth. It was they who ruled the day every day. And thus it was in North Carolina for the first four centuries and three years.

Highlights of the Ticket-Splitter Rebellion of the 1990s

Since 1990, North Carolina's traditionally disenfranchised minority groups capitalized on an era of voter cynicism and rode the shoulders of ticket-splitting revolutionaries into first-time opportunities to wield significant political authority.

North Carolina's 1990s antiestablishment political "firsts" include:

- First woman ever elected to a statewide office
- First Speaker of the House of African American descent
- First Republican Speaker of the House of Representatives in the twentieth century (a Pennsylvanian too!)
- First African American Republicans in state Senate and House since the Reconstruction Era following the Civil War
- First General Assembly with parity of partisan power this century
- First election year this century in which Republicans in either chamber had more money than Democrats (1996 House races)
- First decade in which women chair major legislative committees
- First half-million-dollar campaign for a state legislative district
- First governor with any form of veto power
- First double-digit "Unaffiliated" statewide voter registrations (from 4.9% in 1988 to 13.4% in 1998)
- First time ever Republicans achieve parity in statewide registrations after seven of ten of over a million new registered voters in the 1990s choose not to register as a Democrat.

When the history books are written for future generations of tarheels, the Ticket Splitter Rebellion of the 1990s will be noted as a redefining moment which changed North Carolina's political landscape forever.

The Anatomy of a North Carolina Ticket-Splitter

Declining party loyalty in the early 1990s, especially among traditional Democrats, fueled this decade of profound political change in North Carolina. Early empirical evidence of declining party loyalty can be seen in statewide polling commissioned by NCFREE in 1991 and conducted by Marketing Research Institute, Pensacola, Florida. The following question was asked:

"When it comes to the North Carolina General Assembly, do you think that Democrats can manage state government better, that Republicans can manage state government better, or that political party makes no difference in the ability to manage state government?''

Overwhelmingly North Carolina voters stated that political party made no difference in the ability to manage state government. The table also shows the follow-up results to the same question when asked in a 1995 statewide survey. Throughout the 1990s, it is clear, voters concluded in large numbers that neither party offered partisan solutions to the major concerns of the day that were any better than the other party.

Which Party Manages State Government Better?

	1991 Survey	1995 Survey
Democrats Better	19.1%	14.3%
Republicans Better	16.5	24.6
No Difference	62.4	59.0
Undecided	2.0	2.1

Marketing Research Institute

It is also significant to note that only 2 percent of the voters were uncertain about their answer to this question. They were certain. Party didn't matter.

When, in the course of human events, it becomes necessary for one people to dissolve the political bonds which have connected them with another. . . .
Thomas Jefferson, Declaration of Independence

Necessity is the mother of all political activism.

By 1992, voters throughout America had concluded, after one-too-many broken promises like President Bush's infamous "read my lips, no new taxes" pledge, that it was necessary to change their voting behavior in order to change a political system that had become too complex to understand and too alienated to influence.

Therefore, not knowing how to change the system itself, voters exercised the only option they had: the option to throw the leaders of the system out of office.

Thus began North Carolina's decade-long pattern of antiestablishment voting behavior.

In 1992, 56.4 percent of North Carolina voters joined the rest of the nation in the worst repudiation of a Republican administration since Taft and Hoover by throwing President George Bush out of the White House.

After venting their frustration on the president in 1992, voters returned to predictable behavior and left state and local political leaders alone. However, by 1994, that small dose of over-the-counter political medicine proved to be inadequate. It was now time for the high-powered prescriptions.

In 1994 North Carolina voters unleashed their anger on the entire establishment, federal and state. North Carolinians elected a Republican majority state House of Representatives for the first time in this century, effectively dividing state lawmaking power equally between the two dominant political parties. Titans of traditional power in the North Carolina General Assembly were either thrown out of office or banished to the back row of the uninfluential.

Another century-first result of the antiestablishment ticket-splitter rebellion of 1994 was the election of more Republicans than Democrats in the twelve-member delegation to the U.S House of Representatives. Eight Republicans and four Democrats represented North Carolina in Washington, D.C., from 1995 to 1997.

During the first few months following the 1994 elections, many of North Carolina's leading political pundits joined the chorus of Democrats who declared the recent unpleasantness a one-time fluke driven by low turnout of the traditional Democratic bloc. In an effort to shore up their now-wavering base of financial backers, dethroned Democrat leaders worked frantically to assure the political community that they would be back on the throne in just two short years. Republicans pontificated otherwise. Nobody knew.

In early 1995 political analysts were left to ponder the riddle on most political minds, "Was November 1994 a temporary angry storm or something more like a sea change, something larger and more permanent?"

The following question was posed to North Carolina voters in March 1995 in a statewide poll commissioned by NCFREE and conducted by Dr. Verne Kennedy, Marketing Research Institute, Pensacola, Florida:

''Regardless of how you are registered to vote, do you think of yourself as a Democrat, a Republican or an Independent?''

The results, when compared to the response to the same question asked in 1991, were astounding. North Carolinians who thought of themselves as Republicans or Independent Republicans had not changed even a fraction of one percent. The total of Republicans/ Independent Republicans in North Carolina was 41.4 percent in 1991 and 41.4 percent in March of 1995 despite the fact that Tarheel voters had just elected a twentieth-century first: a Republican-dominated U.S. congressional delegation and state House of Representatives.

The answer to the puzzle becomes clear when you take a look at the Democrat and Independent Democrat results. As you see in the table on page 99, Democrat loyalists plummeted from a 1991 total of 43.3 percent to a 1995 total of 33.2 percent. Loyal Democrats had held their noses in the voting booth and voted for one of "those Republicans" for the state legislature for the first time ever. However, they saved face by not becoming Republicans. These voters either had become Independent ticket-splitting Democrats, willing to vote Republican in a state legislative race just like they had done in statewide and federal races for several decades, or they had become one of the now one-of-four voters who had given up on both parties and had become Independent/Independents.

Remarkably, the poll results showed that 57.7 percent of North Carolina voters said the word "independent" first when asked, "... do you think of yourself as a Democrat, a Republican or an Independent?" The riddle was solved. Ticket-splitters ruled.

North Carolina Political Party Identification

	1991 Survey	1995 Survey
Republican	24.4%	22.8%
Independent Republican	17.0	18.6
Independent	14.5	25.4
Independent Democrat	11.9	13.7
Democrat	31.4	19.5
Total Republican	41.4	41.4
Total Democrat	43.3	33.2

Despite the fact that the 1994 elections were dominated by an antiestablishment mob of ticket-splitting voters seeking to teach the political leaders a lesson, the result in North Carolina was divided power. Republicans for the first time in the twentieth century had an equal place at the public policy table in North Carolina. The consequences of that fact are enormous and long lasting.

The All-New Agenda du Jour

Like metal filings to a magnet, the political affections of the politically dependent flew quickly and unashamedly to the nouveau-powerful Republicans. With the simple banging of the call-to-order-gavel, North Carolina House Republicans, with a 68-to-52-member advantage, declared their Contract with North Carolina the "agenda du jour."

Immediately their prospects for good legislative success in 1995 brightened as North Carolina's community of heretofore Democrat-loyal lobbyists made their rounds to pledge their allegiance and to drop off checks to help pay off campaign debts.

Throughout 1995, North Carolina's left-of-center Democrats were forced by the events of 1994 to join the center-right and sometimes even the right-right. At the July end of the first Republican-led session in this century, Republicans proudly boasted an almost 100 percent success rate with their legislative agenda. Taxes were cut, prisons were added, government was downsized, local control added to public education authority, big spenders were on the run, and the power of the plaintiff lawyers was finally checked at the

99

door of the Republican House Judiciary Committee in charge of the tort reform.

North Carolina's Cul-de-sac Voters — The October Surprise of '95

During the spring of 1996, NCFREE conducted a comprehensive study of voter registration trends in North Carolina. All one hundred county clerks were contacted for the mandated October update of the number of Democrats, Republicans, and Unaffiliated voters in each precinct.

The exceptional value of the mid-decade voter registration study was the fact that North Carolina was experiencing a phenomenal growth of new citizens. Almost three-fourths of a million new voters had registered to vote by October 1995. As the bell sounded in the 1996 Jesse Helms–versus–Harvey Gantt rematch for the U.S. Senate seat, one of every five voters had not been registered when Helms and Gantt fought their first fight in 1990.

The registration study produced astounding results. In a state dominated by Democrats since the Big Bang, 8.3 of every 10 voters who registered in the decade of the 1990s registered either as a Republican or as Unaffiliated.

Restated for emphasis, *83 percent* of all new voters in North Carolina registered either as a Republican or as Unaffiliated from 1990 to 1995. The data showed that Democratic voter growth exceeded Republican and Unaffiliated growth in only one of forty-two state Senate districts and in only four of ninety-eight state House districts.

Permanent revolutionary change had taken place in North Carolina. Republicans and Independents had swamped the Democrats at the registration tables. This meant that the Republican victories of 1994 were not just a one-time violent storm of protest-voters getting even with the establishment Democrats. Something more permanent had been going on.

Republican and Independent registrations were centered in the state's high-growth areas around Raleigh and its high-tech Research Triangle Park; Charlotte and its globally respected banking industry; and Wilmington, with its movie makers, retirees, and port-way to the world. Thousands of cul-de-sacs were being carved in the forested perimeters of North Carolina high-growth cities: cul-de-sacs filled with new upper-income and highly educated voters, many of whom were not raised in the South.

Are You from Dixie?

New North Carolina voters who were not raised in the South were more likely to register as Republicans but, ironically, were not as conservative as most North Carolina Democrats! Republicans raised outside of the South were no more conservative than moderate. They were not antigovernment like many of the more strident populist southern Democrats of the 1990s. These Republicans wanted the best schools and the safest neighborhoods. They wanted lots of soccer fields and city parks and clean lakes and rivers.

The ironic consequence of the new explosion of Republicans in North Carolina in this decade is that the state became less conservative. At the same time traditional North Carolina conservative Democrats began to split their tickets and vote for Republicans, newcomer moderate Republicans were splitting their tickets too and voting for Democrats.

Looking only at the results of GOP-dominated high-growth suburban precincts from the 1996 U.S. Senate race, Democrat Harvey Gantt out-polled Jesse Helms by nearly 60 percent to 40 percent.

North Carolina was changing in ways no one had anticipated.

During the past twenty-five years the percentage of North Carolinians registered as Democrats has plummeted from 73.4 percent to a 1998 low of 52.7 percent. Conversely, North Carolina Republicans have grown from a 1972 total of 22.9 percent to a 1998 all-time high of 33.9 percent. It should also be noted that the percent of Unaffiliated voters tripled in this decade alone, from around 5.5 percent to 13.4 percent, a clear indicator of the mood of the electorate.

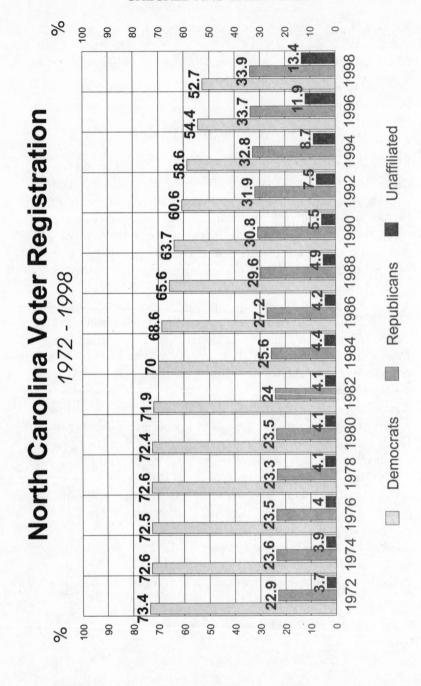

North Carolina Voter Registration
1972 - 1998

Democrats   Republicans   Unaffiliated

On North Carolina Political Scales, 55 Percent and 35 Percent Weigh the Same

The unique significance of 55 percent Democrat registrations and 35 percent Republican registrations is that in North Carolina they are practically equal numbers.

Ten years ago NCFREE discovered that when Republican registration reached 35 percent in legislative districts, Republicans were favored to win. Throughout this decade, Republicans have held over 90 percent of all state legislative seats that are at least 35 percent Republican. This is due to the large number of conservative Democrats who split their tickets and vote for Republican candidates.

Therefore, with a combination of new Republicans and Democrat ticket-splitters, the long-sought GOP goal of party parity had been achieved.

What Hath Antiestablishment Ticket-Splitting Wrought?

By the time the 1996 elections rolled around, the decade of the 1990s had produced three historic political changes: changes that would foretell the results of November 1996 balloting. First, six of ten voters in North Carolina had become independent ticket-splitters. Second, the surge of Republican registrations in the 1990s yielded a level partisan playing field. Democrats no longer enjoyed their traditional advantage. Third, and most important, Republican parity of power in state government, which was handed to them by angry ticket-splitting Democrats in 1994, translated into parity of money.

In North Carolina, money flows to political power. And the candidate with the most money wins 80 percent of the time.

In North Carolina, 1996 was the first election year in this century in which equally capable combatants, Republicans and Democrats, fought on a level playing field with an equal amount of financial backing.

The new dilemma for political operatives was, if no one has an advantage, then how do you win? Almost simultaneously all consultants and purveyors of political wares agreed on the answer.

You win by simply buying something that your opponent does not have.

Not until the mid-1990s did state legislative candidates in North Carolina make congressional-campaign-level strategic expenditures for campaign-budget line items like polling, multiple mass mail, TV ads, opposition research, and, of course, high-priced campaign consultants.

The financial implications of party parity were staggering. The cost of winning a state Senate race grew from a 1994 average of $32,000 to $82,000 in one election cycle. That's a 126 percent increase.

In many states, $82,000 may sound like a bargain. In North Carolina it was outrageous.

The total spent on state legislative races in 1996 was over $14 million, up from $7-plus million in 1994. And the $14 million did not include the several million in the now-infamous soft money of 1996 that meandered its way effortlessly through legal loopholes and poured into North Carolina state legislative campaigns.

North Carolina State Legislative Campaign Spending Skyrockets

	1993–94	1995–96	% Change
All State Senate	$3,205,312	$6,517,173	103%
Senate Winners Only	1,815,066	4,108,118	126
All State House	4,788,840	7,579,406	58
House Winners Only	3,066,084	5,000,604	63
Total — Winners Only	4,881,150	9,108,722	87
Total — All Candidates	7,994,152	14,096,579	76

Ticket-splitters are responsible for parity of power in the North Carolina General Assembly. Parity of power automatically meant parity of money. Parity of money meant that the cost of winning doubled in one election cycle.

The impact of ticket-splitters on North Carolina state legislative politics cannot be overestimated. Ticket-splitters are the El Niño of today's North Carolina political climate.

North Carolina Ticket-Splitters Choose
Divided Government in 1996

Much like the rest of the nation, North Carolinians expressed their ongoing cynicism in 1996 in one of two ways. One, they didn't bother to vote. Two, they split their tickets and chose divided government.

North Carolina voter turnout was the lowest in twenty-five years. Likewise, U.S. voter turnout in 1996 was the lowest since 1924. National TV news coverage of 1996 federal races was down 40 percent compared to the previous presidential campaign year. The percentage of Americans watching the 1996 televised national conventions or the presidential debates was the lowest in the history of TV coverage of those two major political events.

Those who did vote in 1996 followed the now well-established pattern of ticket-splitting and chose a divided, centrist government.

By 1996 Americans had almost completely abandoned the extreme political left. However, by 1996, voters throughout America grew leery of an extreme political right under the leadership of Newt Gingrich.

Polling conducted in August/September 1996 showed that 43 percent of North Carolina's likely voters had a strong unfavorable opinion of Newt Gingrich. Only 29 percent of North Carolinians surveyed had a positive impression of Newt Gingrich.

Like North Carolinians, voters throughout America began to express concerns about a Republican Congress led by too many conservatives demonstrating too little compassion for people in need.

This negative impression was particularly strong among women, most notably among a new bloc in American politics: single white women. In North Carolina, the negative opinion of Newt Gingrich among single white women in 1996 was a whopping 59 percent. Single white women, now mirroring the economic profile of minority women, were voting accordingly.

America had become a nation of two-income households. Single white women, including widows and single moms, were struggling to make ends meet with only one income. Compounding the problem was the fact that women typically earn less than men.

In 1996, single white women abandoned Republicans in droves. The typical gender gap of 5 percent grew to 20 percent and higher.

Led by women, particularly single white women, North Carolinians and the nation backed quickly away from the right and clustered near the philosophical center.

Furthermore, in order to ensure that neither the right nor the left took the nation down any extreme path, voters checked the power of the right and the left by giving both an equal amount of power.

North Carolina is the perfect example of a people intentionally choosing to divide government power. On the same election day in November 1996, the same group of people, North Carolina voters, cast votes that elected the GOP presidential candidate Bob Dole, the Democrat gubernatorial candidate Jim Hunt, the GOP U.S. Senate candidate Jesse Helms, the Democrat slate for all Council of State seats, a Republican state House of Representatives, and a Democrat state Senate, and then split the twelve-member U.S. House delegation right down the middle, six Republicans and six Democrats. That's divided government.

North Carolinians, like all Americans, simply no longer trusted either party with 100 percent of the power.

Ticket-Splitters and Politics
at the Brink of the New Millennium

From a scandal-plagued and arrogant Congress and a visionless Bush presidency to today's morally challenged Clinton administration, voters of the final decade of the second great millennium of the common era have watched an endless parade of political disappointments march down the main streets of our cities and towns.

However, despite ongoing and well-justified cynicism, the politics of 1998 will likely yield a low level of incumbent turnover in North Carolina and elsewhere. Consumer confidence in the economy is so upbeat that the more compelling argument is to maintain the status quo. Besides, most voters suspect that the 1998 challengers are no better than the 1998 incumbents.

Further, months and months of scandal-riddled news resulting from the investigation of President Clinton's extramarital affairs and allegations of foreign contributions for political favors will add to the probability of historic low voter turnout in the November elections of 1998, a phenomenon that traditionally favors incumbents.

Conversely, these very scandals are the yeast of a new political revolution in America which could yield historic high turnout and turnover during the elections of 2000. Necessity drives activism. There is an ever-growing sentiment showing up in public opinion polls that it has now become necessary to move the character and values agenda to the top of the list of public priorities. The great irony of the Clinton administration is that its most important legacy very well could be the restoration of character to the qualifications for the U.S. presidency.

Much like the politics of the early 1990s, voters are fast concluding that the only way to restore people of principle to American politics is to wipe the slate clean and start with a fresh new slate. The timing for those seeking such a dramatic turnover in political leadership has never been more gratuitous. The end of a great one-thousand-year period of human history and the beginning of a new great millennium is the quintessential moment for revolutionary political change.

The number of ticket-splitters in America will likely increase in the millennium-driven political era, a highly charged, volatile environment in which incumbents will be very vulnerable. Fresh faces offering hope for the restoration of integrity in our nation's political institutions will likely trounce those candidates associated with the political establishment of the 1990s. After all, it was the political establishment of the 1990s who struck the fatal blow to integrity in American politics. It was the political establishment of the 1990s who gave party loyalists no option but to split their ticket and choose divided power.

Methodological Summary

L ance Tarrance was in the unique position, being affiliated with the Gallup Organization, to have access to the 1996 national post-election poll data. Gallup researchers phoned those respondents who split their ballot for the presidential candidate of one political party and the candidate for U.S. House of Representatives from another political party. In this follow-up call, respondents were asked if they would be willing to discuss the issue of divided government with a political historian writing a book about the election.

The data set included approximately 170 ticket-splitters, of which 78 agreed to participate with a researcher conducting in-depth explorations of their voting decisions. These individuals were stratified by male and female, and approximated the proportion of the four resulting coalitions of ticket-splitters: Clinton-Republican, Dole-Democrat, Perot-Republican, and Perot-Democrat. The following questions were presented over a two-week period in April 1997, replicating a national focus-group format of thirty individuals who discussed their opinions on divided government for an hour to an hour and a half.

The Gallup Organization has enthusiastically supported this additional research, conducting special tabulations of previous research allowing the authors to present a unique insight into the voting behavior of 1996.

We have further examined ticket-splitting through special tabulations made from the 1996 national post-election survey conducted by Gallup, as well as an October 1997 survey measuring a yearlong evaluation of divided government by ticket-splitters.

Administered In-Depth Interview (IDI) Format

The following questions were used to prompt respondents to discuss their views on divided government:

1. *Many people today say that the voters in the United States live in an era or time of "divided government" or "split control" — that is, when one political party is elected to the White House as President and a different political party is elected to the majority in the U.S. Congress. Some believe that this division of power is a good thing, while others do not. What do you think?*

2. *When someone from another country describes the United States system of government, they usually point out that the U.S. Constitution has two special features to it: (a) "The Separation of Powers" and (b) "Checks and Balances." What does the first feature mean to you today and what does the second mean to you today?*

3. *Do you think in the future we ought to have a "unified, President-centered" political party controlling all of government and then let the voters decide in the next election if they want to keep that party in power?*

4. *Do you agree or disagree that if there is "divided government" — that is, when one political party is elected to the White House as President and another party is elected to the majority in the U.S. Congress — that it signifies a lack of trust in either political party to have full power to govern?*

5. *Do you agree or disagree with the following statement — "I would prefer a government that sometimes acts against my views or wishes than a government that does not act at all"?*

6. *Some people say that when one political party controls all the branches of government — such as both the White House and the Congress — that this unified control will put an end to so-called "gridlock" or political-party stalemate in Washington, D.C.*
Others disagree and say that when there is divided government or shared control of government power that the two political parties then must work

harder to come to an agreement and the voters watch more closely the performance of both parties. Which view comes closest to yours — the first or the second? Why do you think that?

7. *Do you agree or disagree with the following statement — "I think it is important to try to split the control of the government between the two major parties because the problems today are so difficult to understand and that any mistakes in direction could hurt our country's future"?*

8. *Many people make their choice for both the President and for their District Representative to the U.S. Congress based upon their stands on the national problems of the day, such as the economy, taxes, defense and the budget. Others do not see such a connection and vote for President based upon national issues, but make their choice for the District Representative to the U.S. Congress based upon mainly local issues and for help with the personal problems of government. Which connection usually affects your vote for Congress — the national one or the local one? Why?*

9. *One last question. There are also about thirty states in which the Governor is of one political party and the state legislature, in whole or in part, is controlled by another political party. Why do you think that voters split control of their state government today?*

10. *Would you be willing to participate in a television documentary on the subject of divided government, to be produced sometime next year?*

Transcripts of Sample In-Depth Interviews

The following in-depth interviews were conducted during April of 1997. Interviewed were respondents to the 1996 presidential post-election poll conducted by the Gallup Organization who split their ballot in the 1996 presidential election.

Deb • Female, 33 • Michigan • Perot-Democrat

Many people today say that voters in the United States live in an era or time of "divided government" or "split control" — that is, when one political party is elected to the White House as President and a different political party is elected to the majority in the U.S. Congress. Some believe that this division of power is a good thing, while others do not. What do you think?

It's a good thing. I think a lot of people are voting for individuals, for people they have personal contact with, or somebody they know or have followed for a time. They know that person based on their integrity. They're more apt to vote for that person rather than along party lines. In my family, a lot of them have voted Democratic. But that's changing, because a number of them voted for control. Traditionally, in my understanding, it was set up to balance power, and I think that's a good thing. One party control is almost anti-American.

CHECKED AND BALANCED

When someone from another country describes the U.S. system of government, they usually point out that the U.S. Constitution has two special features to it: (a) "The Separation of Powers" and (b) "Checks and Balances." What does the first feature mean to you today, and what does the second mean to you today?

Separation of powers means separating the judicial from the executive. Checks and balances has to do with the balance of power. It's almost necessary to have that kind of separation. Our country was founded on the basis that no one person or individual would have total power. Not even the president of the United States should be above the law.

Do you think in the future we ought to have a "unified, President-centered" political party controlling all of government and then let the voters decide in the next election if they want to keep that party in power?

No. That goes against the grain of being American. You're not supposed to have one person totally in control. This country is too darn diverse.

Do you agree or disagree that if there is "divided government" — that is, when one political party is elected to the White House as President and another party is elected to the majority in the U.S. Congress, that it signifies a lack of trust in either political party to have full power to govern?

Not necessarily a lack of trust. It's almost un-American to even consider it. Maybe people are just too fearful of giving one party too much power.

Do you agree or disagree with the following statement — "I would prefer a government that sometimes acts against my views or wishes than a government that does not act at all."

Agree. The government has to act for everyone, not just for me personally. What's good for the country isn't always going to be good for me.

Some people say that when one political party controls all the branches of government — such as both the White House and the Congress — this unified control will put an end to so-called "gridlock" or political-party stalemate in Washington, D.C. Others disagree and say that when there is divided government or shared control of government power the two political parties then must work harder to come to an agreement and the voters watch more closely the performance of both parties. Which view comes closest to yours — the first or the second? Why do you think so?

The second. I think with a Democrat in the White House and a Republican Congress, the public's going to watch more closely.

Do you agree or disagree with the following statement — "I think it is important to try to split the control of the government between the two major parties because the problems today are so difficult to understand and any mistakes in direction could hurt our country's future."

I think two parties are good. Actually, I think there should be more. There's so much they have to deal with, a multitude of sides that have to be focused on.

Many people make their choice for both the President and for their District Representative to the U.S. Congress based upon their stands on the national problems of the day, such as the economy, taxes, defense, and the budget. Others do not see such a connection and vote for President based upon national issues, but make their choice for the District Representative to the U.S. Congress based upon mainly local issues and for help with the personal problems of government. Which connection usually affects your vote for Congress — the national one or the local one? Why?

Local. Actually, more state for me. The person I voted for for Congress is a Democrat. The man has done an incredible amount for the people in this state for years and years. He's well known to all of us. It didn't matter whether he was Republican or Democrat.

One last question. There are also about 30 states in which the Governor is of one political party and the state legislature, in whole or in part, is controlled by another political party. Why do you think that voters split control of their state government today?

Probably for the same reasons. Checks and balances.

113

Can you tell me a little about yourself?

I'm from Michigan. I'm 33, and single with no kids. I work as a Certified nursing assistant. But I'm in school for my bachelor's in Native American History. My background is Native American. I hope to teach or do tribal histories when I finish.

Why did you vote for Perot?

I liked his ideas of turning the economy around. There are certain aspects of government that have to be run like a business. He's right about the effects on the kids. Native Americans always think about the seven generations ahead of them, that what you're doing now is going to affect the generations ahead of you — he's right about that, you have to keep it in focus.

What about the issues?

For me, it's jobs. The economy is a big one. I know the economy is picking up now. I think it's not so much what anyone did, but what just happened. I'm concerned about the environment. Republicans think more like big business, it doesn't matter as long as we're making money. We can make the money now and worry about cleaning up later. I'm very much pro-choice. That's another problem I have with the Republican candidates.

Now that you've had a chance to think about divided government, do you have an opinion about it?

I'd say it's something that is good and intentional. I'm for checks and balances. It's almost anti-American to have one party controlling everything.

Marshall • Male, 31 • Ohio • Clinton-Republican

Many people today say that voters in the United States live in an era or time of "divided government" or "split control" — that is, when one political party is elected to the White House as President and a different political party is elected to the majority in the U.S. Congress. Some believe that this division of power is a good thing, while others do not. What do you think?

I guess it's a good thing, for the simple fact that if something comes through Congress it should be pretty legitimate before it makes it all the way. I would say that's a good thing.

If it's split control, with a Democrat President and a Republican Congress, such as we have right now, that could be a good thing. I guess sometimes you don't want some things going through too quickly. You want consideration to the pros and the cons of what they might be doing. If you have a unilateral party in the Presidency and in Congress, some things that could be good may not go through at all, and some things that could be bad could go right on through. There are pros and cons to anything that goes through. I think if you have split control, it's more apt to bring out some of the controversy for closer examination.

When someone from another country describes the U.S. system of government, they usually point out that the U.S. Constitution has two special features to it: (a) "The Separation of Powers" and (b) "Checks and Balances." What does the first feature mean to you today, and what does the second mean to you today?

Separation of powers? I'm not familiar with that phrase. I guess it goes along with checks and balances. Things have to be approved through the hierarchy, I would say.

Checks and balances is what I was referring to in the first question. You have some people in politics who are for something, and others who are against it. They kind of have to go back and forth and decide what is best for the majority.

If you have split control, they would be more apt to bring out the pros and cons than if you have unilateral control. An increase of checks and balances.

Do you think in the future we ought to have a "unified, President-centered" political party controlling all *of government and then let the voters decide in the next election if they want to keep that party in power?*

No. I guess that would give them more power, and make it off balance.

115

Do you agree or disagree that if there is "divided government" — that is, when one political party is elected to the White House as President and another party is elected to the majority in the U.S. Congress, it signifies a lack of trust in either political party to have full power to govern?

Somewhat, yes. If you had an all-Democratic government, it might be too easy. Things would go through without a lot of checks and balances. I can see where that would be a problem. Especially now I see the government working differently than what it might have been a few presidencies ago. A lot more things seem to be going through Congress than it used to. If you have an all-Democratic or all-Republican government, I can see a lot of things swimming through that should not.

Do you agree or disagree with the following statement — "I would prefer a government that sometimes acts against my views or wishes than a government that does not act at all."

Agree. My view may be negative as a whole to the country. For example, just because I want an across-the-board income tax at 12%, that may be very good for me. But for someone who may be more at the poverty level, that may not be very good for them. Just because it's good for me, it may not be good for the rest of the country.

Some people say that when one political party controls all the branches of government — such as both the White House and the Congress — this unified control will put an end to so-called "gridlock" or political-party stalemate in Washington, D.C. Others disagree and say that when there is divided government or shared control of government power the two political parties then must work harder to come to an agreement and the voters watch more closely the performance of both parties. Which view comes closest to yours — the first or the second? Why do you think so?

I agree that if you have unified control, you will avoid a lot of stalemates in government; however, I disagree with the premises behind it. With divided control, it makes the two parties work together toward a conclusion. I agree with it. The two parties must work things out and look at the pros and the cons of an issue. As you do that, you may sway the party that was negative toward the issue, you may sway

116

them toward your direction as they see it from a different point of view. Divided government is going to make the voters more aware of what is going on. If he views the issue from a different standpoint than the voters might normally think he would, then he might have to state why he voted as he did. And that can also change the view of voters. I just see it as a more open forum.

Do you agree or disagree with the following statement — "I think it is important to try to split the control of the government between the two major parties because the problems today are so difficult to understand and any mistakes in direction could hurt our country's future."

I wouldn't necessarily say any mistakes. I do agree with that. It goes back to the checks and balances. If you're talking big international decisions, or anything of that nature, it's important that both parties agree or come to the best decision for what is best for the country.

Many people make their choice for both the President and for their District Representative to the U.S. Congress based upon their stands on the national problems of the day, such as the economy, taxes, defense, and the budget. Others do not see such a connection and vote for President based upon national issues, but make their choice for the District Representative to the U.S. Congress based upon mainly local issues and for help with the personal problems of government. Which connection usually affects your vote for Congress — the national one or the local one? Why?

The local one. Those people are more in touch with what's going on in this state. When they assemble into Congress, they have become more unified in making larger decisions for the United States. So I vote for a Congressman based on the local issues and that specific Congressman has his view of how things are going in my state, and he can bring that to the Congress as a whole.

One last question. There are also about 30 states in which the Governor is of one political party and the state legislature, in whole or in part, is controlled by another political party. Why do you think that voters split control of their state government today?

That I'm not sure. I can see where that would be a problem. A lot of the state issues, you're dealing with smaller issues. I think you'd want the issues to go through a little smoother.

Tell me about yourself and your family.

I live in Westerville, Ohio, a northern suburb of Columbus. I'm married, with one son, 11. I'm a sonographer, I do ultrasounds. My wife works in nuclear medicine. Economy is treating them pretty good. Being in the medical field, we have a lot of buy-outs. We were acquired by a larger hospital. We're doing all right, though the raises don't come as frequently as I'd like to see them. My wife works because we need her to. She probably doesn't need to work full time, she could probably work part-time.

What issues are of interest to you?

Health care reform was a big one for us. We realized something does need to be done in health care. Mr. and Mrs. Clinton went at it kind of gung-ho in the beginning, and maybe not in the best of ways. But I still think they will try to do something in health care. Somebody's going to have to. And they're the only people I've heard talk about it. Being as close as I am to it, I know it's screwed up. There is no quick fix. That swayed how we voted.

Why did you vote the way you did?

To be honest, I was not impressed with Bob Dole. Some of his ideology, and he just didn't strike me as someone I'd want to put in that position.

Do you consider yourself a Republican or a Democrat?

I would consider myself more Republican. Just for local issues. In the past, I did strictly vote Republican. My wife and I did discuss the last election, and while Clinton was in office, it's been okay. I guess I was kind of afraid to make a change to Bob Dole. We knew what we had.

Now that you've had a chance to think about divided government, do you have an opinion about it?

I don't think I intentionally voted for divided government. I can see what I did was a good thing, and in retrospect I think it is a good thing. But I don't think I intentionally did that. If the Republican Party would have had a more attractive candidate, I very well probably would have voted Republican. But split control may not be such a bad thing. I think you've brought to the surface a lot of things I really hadn't thought about. It's not a bad thing, split control.

Have you seen more effective government or legislation with it?

Yes and no. We talked about stalemate. I think we have a more aggressive government. Maybe things don't get done as quickly, but it's making them work at it. Legislation is better.

John • Male, 34 • Arizona • Clinton-Republican

Many people today say that voters in the United States live in an era or time of "divided government" or "split control" — that is, when one political party is elected to the White House as President and a different political party is elected to the majority in the U.S. Congress. Some believe that this division of power is a good thing, while others do not. What do you think?

I think it's a good thing. I'm not a political or history student. It seems that whenever the White House and the Congress are controlled by the same party, one of two things happen. There's either nothing. Nothing happens. Stagnation. Or there's really radical change, legislatively. Our country doesn't seem to fare well under either of those two scenarios.

When someone from another country describes the U.S. system of government, they usually point out that the U.S. Constitution has two special features to it: (a) "The Separation of Powers" and (b) "Checks and Balances." What does the first feature mean to you today, and what does the second mean to you today?

The separation of powers means the people who make the laws aren't the people who administer the laws. And the people who

119

administer the laws aren't the people who mete out justice. Checks and balances is the product of having the division of power. Having a division of power provides checks and balances so that one portion or group of people aren't enabled to become too powerful.

Do you think in the future we ought to have a "unified, President-centered" political party controlling all *of government and then let the voters decide in the next election if they want to keep that party in power?*

No. I'm not a party man, myself. But occasionally I will vote according to party lines if I'm not real familiar with the candidate. I think that having multiple parties is beneficial, just like I think it's beneficial to have two places to go buy hamburger. It provides motivation to provide the best for the most.

Do you agree or disagree that if there is "divided government" — that is, when one political party is elected to the White House as President and another party is elected to the majority in the U.S. Congress, it signifies a lack of trust in either political party to have full power to govern?

Not as far as I'm concerned. For instance, I don't really care which party is in power in either case. I prefer that we have a divided government. I don't think it necessarily shows a distrust. . . . I never thought about why it happens. But in my case, no, it's not. It's not a matter of distrust of either.

Do you agree or disagree with the following statement — "I would prefer a government that sometimes acts against my views or wishes than a government that does not act at all."

Absolutely. Why? Well, first off, I could be wrong! If I'm not, there's going to be enough people with my opinion that doing something wrong may galvanize them to become vocal. Whereas if everything is status quo, it's basic physics. An object at rest won't stay that way. A lot of people, including myself, need some sort of motivation. Sometimes seeing something really stupid is a good motivator.

Some people say that when one *political party controls* all *the branches of government — such as both the White House and the Congress — this unified control will put an end to so-called "gridlock" or political-party stalemate in Washington, D.C.*

I've seen it happen where things have gotten through a lot quicker. Things that would not have gotten through. Decisions that were made that would not have been made had there been a divided government. I'm not sure that really is the question you're asking. I think the question you're asking is, Is that a good thing? Does it facilitate government? If that's the question you're asking, no, I don't think it does. I think it facilitates . . . it could be, it could be a vehicle for good for government. It all depends on what is getting sent through. I hate to be cynical, but most of the time it's a pork-barrel thing. You give me this, and I'll get you that, and we'll both get rich.

Others disagree and say that when there is divided government or shared control of government power the two political parties then must work harder to come to an agreement and the voters watch more closely the performance of both parties. Which view comes closest to yours — the first or the second? Why do you think so?

Wholeheartedly. Just because of the fact that there is disagreement, that gives the media something to report on, that puts it in the faces of people who would look for it. If everything is going smoothly, it's not news most of the time. It's only when there's contention. Having a divided government provides contention. It also provides a way to motivate both the executive and the judicial and the legislative branches to know that they're going to have to defend themselves and put their best foot forward.

The political climate changes, but politicians — the ones that last, for the most part — are the ones that don't do so much finger-pointing as much as acting. This is what our political party has done. That's what they did that was bad. Here's what we did that was good. If you look at the icons of politics . . . Barry Goldwater, I think is an excellent example. He rarely talks bad about the Democrats. You hear him badmouth the Republicans more often than the Democrats. I think him and people like him try to further their political party by motivating them to do their best to serve the people. I really do believe there are plenty of politicians out there who really truly want to do that, if only because that's there job and they really want to be good at it. In order to do that they have to do what's best. In order to do that, they really need to come up with things that are good for the people.

Do you agree or disagree with the following statement — "I think it is important to try to split the control of the government between the two major parties because the problems today are so difficult to understand and any mistakes in direction could hurt our country's future."

No. I think our future is really forgiving. I think we could really goof up and it wouldn't be catastrophic. I would like to point out that I think bright individuals exist not just in Republicans and Democrats, but in libertarian and some of the less common parties. People should be seen for the merit of their ideas, not necessarily for the party they belong to.

Many people make their choice for both the President and for their District Representative to the U.S. Congress based upon their stands on the national problems of the day, such as the economy, taxes, defense, and the budget. Others do not see such a connection and vote for President based upon national issues, but make their choice for the District Representative to the U.S. Congress based upon mainly local issues and for help with the personal problems of government. Which connection usually affects your vote for Congress — the national one or the local one? Why?

Local. Just because they're supposed to be representing the people of this area in a federal situation. Yes, they have to deal with the national issues and international issues, so they'd better be well-versed on that as well. But if they're not in touch with me as a voter and as an occupant of the district they're in, how can they possibly know what's going to be good for me or my area.

One last question. There are also about 30 states in which the Governor is of one political party and the state legislature, in whole or in part, is controlled by another political party. Why do you think that voters split control of their state government today?

I didn't know that. I don't know. Quite possibly for the same reasons of not allowing one party to control, which would, in my opinion, either allow rampant strange laws or just status quo.

Can you tell me a little about yourself? For example, do you have a family?

No, I don't have a family. I'm 34 years old. Divorced with two teenage boys.

You do have a family.

Yeah. The youngest one will turn 13 in a couple days. The older is 15. They live in a different town than I do. I get to see them every couple of weeks. I'm still on good terms with my ex-wife. In fact, we get along better now than before.

I became a plumber for a couple of years. Then I went back to school. I kept waiting till I could afford to go back to school. Then, finally, my best friend explained to me, you know John, you can't wait till you can afford it. And I said, Dan, you're right. So I went, and got my four-year degree at Arizona State University — the best eight years of my life — in electronic engineering technology.

I work at Hughes Missile Systems company.

Are you politically inclined?

I do try to pay attention to what's going on, catch the five o'clock news.

How is the economy treating you?

In the early 80s I was young, I had a family already. It was pretty miserable for a couple years there. People badmouth him a lot, Reagan, but my quality of life just got three to four hundred percent better. Looking back on it, what he did didn't make any sense, but it seemed to work in my personal experience.

Would you talk to me about your 96 vote?

I wanted that division of government. When it became obvious that the Congress was going to be Republican, and it looked like, watching the polls, both House and Senate were going to be controlled by Republicans . . . I kind of like it when the Congress is even divided. The Senate is Republican, say, and the House is Democrat. I do notice what you end up with is watered-down laws.

But I did like the idea of having a Democrat in the executive branch because he gets to choose the judges.

I am registered as a Republican, and I seem to line up more with their positions. But there are a lot of "democratic" policies and ideas that appeal to me. I like the idea of society taking care of its own people. There was a time when this country didn't need that. When Grandma got old, you cleaned out a room and that's where she lived. And she watched the kids after school. I see that as something the government could take action on, and the Democrats more willing to do that than the Republicans.

One of the things I thought Bill did well was initiate the college repayment, allowing college graduates to repay their loan by contributing to their communities. I think any motivation to give people to invest in their communities will make them stronger. We are but a collection of communities.

When I voted, several states had already been reported on. And it looked like Bill Clinton was going to win. I nearly voted for Dole anyway. Just because I didn't want Bill to win by much. I didn't want him to think we were extremely happy with him. I'm just one of millions, but it's a way of expressing my opinion. Okay, I definitely want divided government, but I don't want you to think everything's all rosy. You barely made it, buddy.

Do you see more effective legislation with divided control?

I don't know about effective legislation, but I think the laws that have come out are of higher quality than before. But it's hard to get them to do anything. But that's the situation you have with most any product. If you want a nice one, it's going to take time.

Darlene • Female, 66 • Illinois • Perot/Republican

Many people today say that voters in the United States live in an era or time of "divided government" or "split control" — that is, when one political party is elected to the White House as President and a different political party is elected to the majority in the U.S. Congress. Some believe that this division of power is a good thing, while others do not. What do you think?

It probably is a good thing. But my main feeling is it doesn't make any difference as long as the people you send are good people. I don't think it should make any difference party-wise. If you have a president of one party, and the Congress of the other, at least it's a checkmate. And many times it's a stumbling block because they never seem to get anything done.

When someone from another country describes the U.S. system of government, they usually point out that the U.S. Constitution has two special features to it: (a) "The Separation of Powers" and (b) "Checks and Balances." What does the first feature mean to you today, and what does the second mean to you today?

Separation of powers means the states are to a degree independent of the federal government. Checks and balances — people from one party being in Congress and the president being of another. Even though it seems like they don't get a lot done, with one party in power, they could just steamroll right on through everything they wanted to do.

Do you think in the future we ought to have a "unified, President-centered" political party controlling all of government and then let the voters decide in the next election if they want to keep that party in power?

Nothing about Great Britain's system would I want. They don't seem to do any better than we do. With all our problems we still seem to have the best system. We just need people that are more knowledgeable about the people they put into office.

Do you agree or disagree that if there is "divided government" — that is, when one political party is elected to the White House as President and another party is elected to the majority in the U.S. Congress, it signifies a lack of trust in either political party to have full power to govern.

I think it depends more on who's running. Not a lack of trust.

Do you agree or disagree with the following statement — "I would prefer a government that sometimes acts against my views or wishes than a government that does not act at all."

125

I agree. I certainly would prefer one that acted against something I didn't like than one that never got off first base to do anything. You can't make progress if you have inactivity.

Some people say that when one political party controls all the branches of government — such as both the White House and the Congress — this unified control will put an end to so-called "gridlock" or political-party stalemate in Washington, D.C. Others disagree and say that when there is divided government or shared control of government power the two political parties then must work harder to come to an agreement and the voters watch more closely the performance of both parties. Which view comes closest to yours — the first or the second? Why do you think so?

I favor the second. I think the voters do watch more carefully. Here in Illinois we have the situation with the Governor of one party and the legislature being another. It seems like they were gridlock. But the people just got so fed up that they came down hard on their legislators and they were forced to do something. Later that gridlock ends. There are many checks and balances with having that sort of thing.

Do you agree or disagree with the following statement — "I think it is important to try to split the control of the government between the two major parties because the problems today are so difficult to understand and any mistakes in direction could hurt our country's future."

Agree. If you make a big mistake, it can affect the whole world, what we do in this country. I think having divided government, even if you have gridlock once in a while, it's a good check and balance.

Many people make their choice for both the President and for their District Representative to the U.S. Congress based upon their stands on the national problems of the day, such as the economy, taxes, defense, and the budget. Others do not see such a connection and vote for President based upon national issues, but make their choice for the District Representative to the U.S. Congress based upon mainly local issues and for help with the personal problems of government. Which connection usually affects your vote for Congress — the national one or the local one? Why?

I think the national one more. Their views nationally are very important. It affects not only the state, but nationally and also the world.

One last question. There are also about 30 states in which the Governor is of one political party and the state legislature, in whole or in part, is controlled by another political party. Why do you think that voters split control of their state government today?

I can only say how I feel. I think the popularity of the people involved have a lot to do with it, especially at the local level.

Tell me a little about yourself.

I'm divorced, with three grown children and three grandchildren. I work part-time with a CPA firm. I live on a lake outside Petersburg, Illinois.

What issues are important to you?

Cloning. I'm worried about the influx of people who come into our country that are not supposed to be here.

Why did you vote for Perot?

I don't like Bill Clinton. I don't trust him. I said if the Republicans had run anybody else, I would have voted for them.
    One thing the Republican party had against them was their stand on abortion. I think every woman should have a choice. I resent the 60- or 70-year-old men in Congress saying you can't do that. I resent that very much. I think that was a hot political issue, and the Republican party relied too much on the Moral Majority and they got beat.
    I think the entitlement programs now are just out-of-hand. And our national debt absolutely has to be addressed, no matter how unpopular it is.

"Before our interview today, you likely had not given much thought to the idea of divided government or shared control. Now that you've had some time to explore your thoughts, what is your overall impression?"

127

I would lean toward that more. When there is a good program, you have to work hard to get it through. And that's good. Programs that are put through government should be looked at hard and long. If you have someone of the opposite party, they're going to tear it apart if they can, so that if it finally makes it through and becomes the law, at least it's been done thoroughly.

I think it's happening more. Because of the great national debt we owe and the last election, they came to realize they have to work harder to work together to do something. I think the time has passed that they vote something down just along party lines. But the pressure will be on more and more to get away from that and do what is best for the people. I think the people in this country are pretty fed up.

Do you consider yourself a Republican or a Democrat?

That's hard to answer because I'm so damn liberal about so many things, but I would probably lean toward the things the Republicans want to do money-wise because their programs would help me. Liberal on social issues, and fiscally conservative? That's a good way to sum it up.

Richard • Male, 51 • Indiana • Clinton-Republican

Many people today say that voters in the United States live in an era or time of "divided government" or "split control" — that is, when one political party is elected to the White House as President and a different political party is elected to the majority in the U.S. Congress. Some believe that this division of power is a good thing, while others do not. What do you think?

I don't have a strong feeling one way or the other. I see advantages and disadvantages, honestly. Disadvantages are the roadblocks that seem to come along. The advantages, the checks and balances that we don't take wild swings one way or the other.

When someone from another country describes the U.S. system of government, they usually point out that the U.S. Constitution has two special features to it: (a) "The Separation of Powers" and (b) "Checks and Balances." What does the first feature mean to you today, and what does the second mean to you today?

Separation of powers: There are distinct roles in the legislative, judicial and executive branches that are separate and unique and ought to stay that way. Checks and balances: Within any system of governance there ought to be a few guarantees to make sure no single branch has overriding power.

Do you think in the future we ought to have a "unified, President-centered" political party controlling all of government and then let the voters decide in the next election if they want to keep that party in power?

No. I'm satisfied with the 200-plus years of tradition in American governance that the system works well; it provides some flexibility for the voter to make decisions.

Do you agree or disagree that if there is "divided government" — that is, when one political party is elected to the White House as President and another party is elected to the majority in the U.S. Congress, it signifies a lack of trust in either political party to have full power to govern?

That's certainly not what my vote meant, so I guess I would say no. I was voting more for the person. The choices I made, while I was not wildly enthusiastic in every case, was the best choice of the two or three names that were on the ballot at any given time. I certainly am frustrated at the seeming inability of folks not to work together, and to put partisan politics behind them once they're in office, but we'll have to find a different way to resolve that current shortcoming of our current elected officials.

Do you agree or disagree with the following statement — "I would prefer a government that sometimes acts against my views or wishes than a government that does not act at all."

Agree. I can respect a person who tells me they're going to run on a certain platform, and, even though I didn't vote for them, continue to fulfill that platform when elected. I guess I have enough confidence in the democratic process that I think that's the way the system is supposed to work. Four years later, or two years later, I'll "seek my revenge" and see if I can influence the direction the other way. Generally speaking, I think it's better to act than not, and have some policy moved forward.

Some people say that when one *political party controls* all *the branches of government — such as both the White House and the Congress — this unified control will put an end to so-called "gridlock" or political-party stalemate in Washington, D.C. Others disagree and say that when there is divided government or shared control of government power the two political parties then must work harder to come to an agreement and the voters watch more closely the performance of both parties. Which view comes closest to yours — the first or the second? Why do you think so?*

I agree with both statements. My perception would be, in the course of history, I'm sure there have been times when our country has been well served by unanimity of the Presidency and Congress, and times when it's been well-served by division. I think there are valid arguments for both.

Do you agree or disagree with the following statement — "I think it is important to try to split the control of the government between the two major parties because the problems today are so difficult to understand and any mistakes in direction could hurt our country's future."

Disagree. It sounds as if the statement has a certain rigidity to it. Certainly government is complex, although society is complex. I guess I'm not overly impressed that it is so complex and so complicated that it's unmanageable.

Many people make their choice for both the President and for their District Representative to the U.S. Congress based upon their stands on the national problems of the day, such as the economy, taxes, defense, and the budget. Others do not see such a connection and vote for President based upon national issues, but make their choice for the District Representative to the U.S. Congress based upon mainly local issues and for help with the personal problems of government. Which connection usually affects your vote for Congress — the national one or the local one? Why?

130

National, unless I have occasion to have some personal familiarity with the local candidates. Then, I guess I'm making my decision more on the person and what the person stands for, and sometimes that's shaded by political issues, and sometimes by others.

One last question. There are also about 30 states in which the Governor is of one political party and the state legislature, in whole or in part, is controlled by another political party. Why do you think that voters split control of their state government today?

In our state, the House is one and the Senate is another. I see a lot of the local decisions as being made more and more by the fact that people have some familiarity with the representatives from this district.

Tell me a little about yourself.

I'm in educational administration at a university in Indiana. I have a wife and two daughters, ages 26 and 18.

What issues motivated you in the last election?

I was concerned about issues related to the way less-well-off citizens in our society were being treated. That was probably the overwhelming issue of concern.

Why did you vote for Clinton and a Republican House member?

I voted for Clinton because I felt closer to his political views, not particularly close to his personal lifestyle or the choices he made. Locally, I voted for a Republican for Congress because I know the Congressman, and felt he was a very effective state legislator; believe he's a man of high principle and is the type of person that would always do what he thought was right. I know him to be an honorable, trustworthy, and intelligent person. And, frankly, I didn't have that familiarity with the Democratic candidate.

Now that you've had a chance to think about divided government, do you have an opinion about it?

I was intrigued by your concept that it is a calculated move on the part of the American electorate to provide checks and balances, not recognizing the Constitution already has them in place. I would not necessarily have given the American electorate that much of a vote of confidence. Generally speaking, all things being equal, I think we would be better off if there were some unanimity in the White House and the Congress, but I'm not displeased with the thought of different views and checks and balances that are created even beyond the Constitutional checks and balances that might be in place. I'm just frustrated that rather than working to govern, we spend a lot of time working to divide. It seems to be like that in the sound bites we get on the news. It's a game-scoring kind of approach to governance as opposed to an issue of the best interest of the people.

What can be done to make it better?

Less political rhetoric and more in-depth discussion of issues. Less seeming emotion or overstatement, and more approaching of issues as we are trying to come to a resolution, and getting on with a decision and letting the chips fall where they may.